MODEL RAILROADING
with JOHN ALLEN

BY LINN H. WESTCOTT

PHOTOGRAPHY BY JOHN ALLEN

EDITOR: BOB HAYDEN
ART DIRECTOR: LAWRENCE LUSER
COPY EDITOR: BURR ANGLE
EDITORIAL ASSISTANT: MARCIA STERN

© 1981 by Linn H. Westcott. All rights reserved. This book may not be reproduced in part or in whole without written permission from the publisher, except in the case of brief quotations used in reviews. Published by Kalmbach Publishing Co., 21027 Crossroads Circle, Waukesha, WI 53187. Printed in U.S.A. Library of Congress Catalog Card Number: 81-80290. ISBN: 0-89024-298-4.

Originally published in paperback, 1981. Second printing, 1982. Third printing, 1989. First hardcover printing, 1996.

Foreword

In a space roughly 24 by 32 feet, John Allen built a model railroad that became one of the best known in the world. His Gorre & Daphetid Railroad was a work of art, and as with any great masterpiece, every time I saw it I discovered things that had been there before but which I had not noticed. Some features were nostalgic, some funny, a few eccentric, but the overall effect was a wonderful land of mountains, cliffs, bridges, cities, lights, clouds, great distances, and, of course, trains. Not so obvious to his visitors, but just as important to John, was the way the system was operated according to railroad rules with the help of a few friends under the strict scrutiny of the master.

To properly understand a model railroad such as John Allen's you should become acquainted with its builder. So that you may, some of this book dwells upon John himself, a fascinating, often quizzical person. He was an accomplished professional photographer who, through the wise investment of a small inheritance, was eventually able to devote more and more of his time to the things he most wanted to do, among them, model railroading. He never married, lived modestly, and kept a well-organized if not meticulous household.

Although he kept up extensive correspondence with many friends and could express himself well, John did not particularly enjoy writing for large audiences. His articles for model railroad magazines here and abroad usually consisted of a brief typed introduction and an ample supply of top-quality photographs with extensive captions. At my suggestion, he toyed with the idea of writing a book. He went so far as to outline the subjects and to make some special photographs, but made no substantial progress before his death in 1973. In January 1969 he wrote to me: "As I may have told you, one time when we were discussing the possibility of a book by me, I would only want to do one if it could be aimed toward showing the thoughtful and educated non-model railroader what our hobby might be about."

I agree heartily, and I like to think that the book you have in your hands is the book John Allen might have written himself. In it, I hope to accomplish three purposes which overlap only slightly: To show what model railroading is about, to describe in detail one of the finest model railroads ever built, and to reveal some of the fascinating personality of John Allen.

I am especially happy that much of this text is in John's own words, quoted from his letters and tapes to friends and from the material he sent to the model railroad magazines. Where his typed or handwritten manuscript was available, I have usually quoted from this original rather than from the edited story that appeared in print. Likewise, almost all of the photographs are John's own. Although his model railroad was destroyed by fire only a few days after he died, John had taken photographs of it at every stage of construction. Some prints and slides were smoke-coated or singed around the edges, but most survived in usable condition. They made this book possible.

Many of John's friends contributed to this book. I am especially grateful to John's brother, Andrew Allen, for making John's correspondence files and photographs available. John told friends little about his family background, so most of my information about John's early life comes from Andrew. Kiyo Yamazaki of *TMS*, the pioneer model railroad magazine of Japan; Hal Carstens of *Railroad Model Craftsman*; and Jim King and Russ Larson of MODEL RAILROADER, my alma mater magazine, graciously made some of John's published photographs available. Andy Sperandeo of the MODEL RAILROADER staff furnished detailed first-hand reminiscences of his operating sessions on the Gorre & Daphetid. Thanks to all of you.

Before it was known that John's own photos would be available, several modelers offered the use of their color slides of the Gorre & Daphetid. With only one or two exceptions, this book is illustrated with John's photos, but thanks go, all the same, to these generous and helpful friends: George Cockle, Jerry Drake, and Don Mitchell. In addition, Jerry Braet was especially helpful in compiling a list of all of John's published articles.

Once a week, the "G.D. Operators" gathered at John's home to run his railroad. At any one time the group was hardly more than half a dozen persons, yet over the years more than a hundred servicemen from military bases near Monterey, California, neighbors, friends, and visiting model railroaders took a turn at the throttles of the Gorre & Daphetid Railroad. My spe-

cial thanks go to several of them who have related their experiences to me. Each is introduced as he is quoted in the following pages.

Linn H. Westcott
Elm Grove, Wisconsin
July 1980

John Allen, the "Wizard of Monterey," as he looked in the late 1960s.

As we first enter John Allen's magical model railroad realm, we glimpse this view of his railroad, a busy river city quite aptly named "Port."

"There is a little thing called imagination which must play an important part on any model railroad."

Meet John Allen and his Gorre & Daphetid Railroad

THE G·D LINE

SUPPOSE just for a moment that the year is 1972, and come along with me to meet John Allen of Monterey, California, and his model railroad, the Gorre & Daphetid. Our visit begins with a phone call, because, like most of us, John did not like it if a person knocked on his front door unexpectedly. Knowing how much John appreciates good eating, we make a date to have dinner with him at one of the fine seafood restaurants along Monterey's famous "Cannery Row" before driving up to the house to see his layout.

The conversation at the dinner table might begin with model railroading, which John always liked to discuss, but often he would steer the talk to other subjects. You might learn that he liked to play badminton and to swim in the surf. He especially liked to talk about economics, but almost any subject would do.

John Allen was a rounded, usually chubby fellow exactly six feet tall. I think I do neither man a disservice to recount that some acquaintances called John Allen "the Orson Welles of model railroading," and certainly there was some resemblance, both physically and intellectually. Others likened John to a big bear, and when kidding friends dubbed him the "Great Poo-bah," he found it difficult to hide the hint of a grin. Occasionally he would diet and slim down, but that would not last long with good food always available at Monterey's numerous fine restaurants.

John dressed informally most of the time, so informally that it took conservative people a little while to discover the diamond personality behind the rough appearance. John himself was quite conservative, but he had no desire to conform to what he considered superficial custom or pretense.

On the drive from Cannery Row to the house our conversation continues. John was never without words unless he was operating his railroad. However, he might not mention, as the car turns from Cannery Row onto Irving Street, that the little white house on the right, about as narrow but longer than a mobile home, was where he used to live and where his first "Gorre & Daphetid" model railroad was built. Like many others, when I first saw the G.D.'s full name in print, I didn't pronounce "gory and defeated" properly, and so missed the post-battle pun until I asked about it. "I thought it was funny, once," John said, "but people get tired of cute names for model railroads and now I'm stuck with it."

John was born in 1913 and spent much of his childhood in Joplin, Missouri. He attended the University of California at Los Angeles, studying economics, then art, and finally photography, which became his profession. He didn't like hot weather, and when he became able to choose any place to live, he chose Monterey. This small city is south of San Francisco and fronts to the north on Monterey Bay, enjoying cool weather most of the year. It would be an even colder and foggier place except for the high pine-covered ridge to the west that protects Monterey's beautiful homes from raw ocean winds. Over the ridge, beside the ocean, are the towns of Carmel and Pebble Beach, the latter with its well-known golf course.

A house on a downhill slope. —— If you want a basement in California, where few homes have them, you might look for a street that bends around a very steep hill and pick a house on the downhill side. That is the kind of location John

In this 1966 self-portrait the engine facilities at Great Divide are in the foreground, while the passenger terminal is behind John.

Allen chose for his home. Cielo Vista Terrace in Monterey is about a mile southwest of downtown, perched halfway up the east slope of the ridge that shields the community from the Pacific.

After turning left onto Cielo Vista Terrace, we drive a quarter mile bending southward around the steep hillside to reach the Allen home near the end of the cul-de-sac. The house is hidden behind overgrown shrubbery. Even though the steep drop-off allows a shallow front lawn, John has let the front yard grow in dense bushes rather than have to mow it.

The modest and attractive redwood house extends parallel to the street with a short steep driveway sloping down to the carport at the right, or south, end. The front door, near the center, is all but hidden in vines. Only the bath and the guest bedroom, to the left, open their windows to the bushy front yard; the main rooms have larger windows opening to the view at the rear.

To the left of the carport we duck through a short tunnel of dangling vines to reach the front door. Inside it is cold, so cold that John's model railroad crew, the G.D. operators, wear thick clothing when running the trains. To the left of the entry a narrow hall leads past the bath to the two bedrooms in the north end of the house, one for guests, one for John. The living room is straight ahead. If we walk across to the east-facing windows, we can look down a steep slope into the tops of the pine trees below.

A long, narrow balcony extends along the rear wall outside of the living room windows. Due to the steepness of the slope, the ground is far below and covered with vines and bushes. The view is great, especially at sunrise when the rays of light filter through the pine and eucalyptus trees of the opposite ridge. Only a few other homes can be seen across the valley. The freeway is mostly hidden by trees in the chasm below, so we hear it more than see it.

From the north wall of the living room a huge photograph of an eye stares at us, a work saved from John's student days in art school. On the right, behind the davenport and along the south wall of the living room, a narrow stairway leads to the basement. Hundreds of model railroad visi-

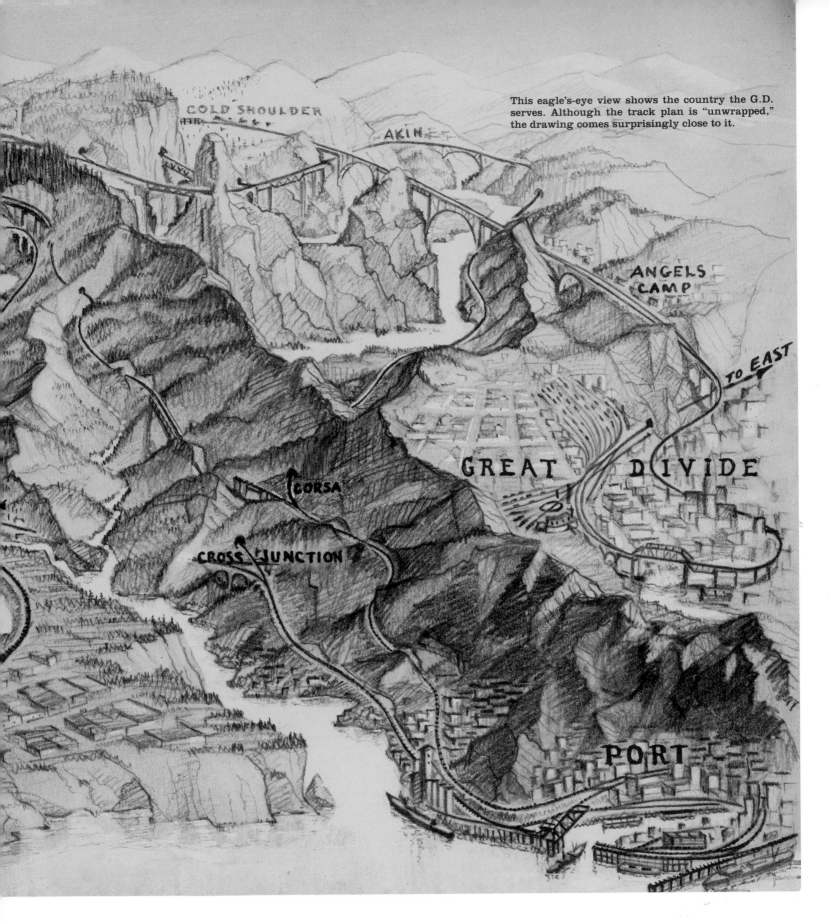

COLD SHOULDER

AKIN

This eagle's-eye view shows the country the G.D. serves. Although the track plan is "unwrapped," the drawing comes surprisingly close to it.

ANGELS CAMP

TO EAST

GREAT DIVIDE

CORSA

CROSS JUNCTION

PORT

tors have descended there since John started his present layout in 1954.

The concept of the Gorre & Daphetid. —— If you are the sort of reader I am, you may have already paged through this book and gathered some idea of what the Gorre & Daphetid looked like. Maybe you have studied the track plan a little, too. If you are an old-timer in model railroading you remember the photographs of the railroad appearing in the model railroad magazines. In any case, let's learn more about it. In

In the highest reaches of G.D. country towns are accessible only by foot, horse, or the railroad. Here, at "Drains," a freight train clings to the steep mountainside.

Squawbottom, located deep in a mountain pass, is the lowest point on the G.D. Trains arrive here with brakes smoking, and take water before assaulting the 3.5 percent upgrade.

this and following chapters we'll learn about the concept of the G.D., and then become acquainted with the various places on the system. We'll do that in the order a train reaches them, but with attention more on the lay of the land than the movements of the train. After that, we'll learn more about John, his first railroads, how the present layout was planned and built, how it is operated, and some of John's humorous antics and serious ideas about model railroading.

Let's suppose you and I and three or four others, including a couple of John's operators, are in the living room chatting with him. A good way to start is to ask about his concept for the railroad. John has an answer ready: "There is a little thing called imagination which must play an important part on any model railroad, but for a tiny one like the first G.D. that I built in the old house, it's imperative. The G.D. concept began there and has been expanded here.

"In my land of make-believe, a whole empire with mergers, celebrations, swindles, and depressions are indulged in.

"A train starts out with cargoes and has places to deliver them. It puffs and works its way around the tortuous curves and dangerous grades, through expensive powder-blasted tunnels and backbreaking cuts. It labors its way through passes where a shooting war with a competing narrow gauge railroad was once fought to gain the right of way.

"This pike is conceived as one division of a railroad through the Akinbak Mountains. The period is the latter days of the steam locomotive era. It is free-lanced, but I suppose the nearest prototype would be the Colorado Midland if the C.M. had continued running into the late 1940s. My G.D. railroad is a bridge line through the mountains and not too prosperous. Lack of auto roads through these passes leaves the area uncluttered with the impedimenta of our modern civilization.

"The railroad is principally a freight line, but due to the scenic grandeur of the Akinbak Mountains, through Giant Canyon and Devil's Gulch, it does have some modern passenger cars for the transcontinental trade that routes itself through this way. Local passenger service uses relatively old equipment.

"The locomotive roster is quite varied with engines purchased secondhand from numerous other railroads while they were dieselizing. The G.D. has no diesels but does operate a gas-electric car. Some ancient equipment is maintained on the roster for use for movie productions.

"The area depicted on the layout is one division beginning at Great Divide and running west through two mountain ranges to Gorre. Great Divide is a division point and the largest city in the area. There is a small classification yard and engine terminal servicing both coal and oil-burning locos. The city is served also by the Cooper Electric trolley line."

The first mountain range is quite high, topped with snowsheds. Beyond the summit the line clings high on the sides of deep canyons as it descends to the halfway city of Port where the G.D. Line interchanges freight and passengers with river boats. Port as a city lacks planning, so has an

This pair of photos shows the Sims Loop steel trestle, near the town of Squawbottom, from above and below. This bridge is located on the sharpest curve on the G.D. main line, and the speed limit here is only 25 miles per hour. John took the low-level view by aiming his camera into a mirror carefully positioned on the floor.

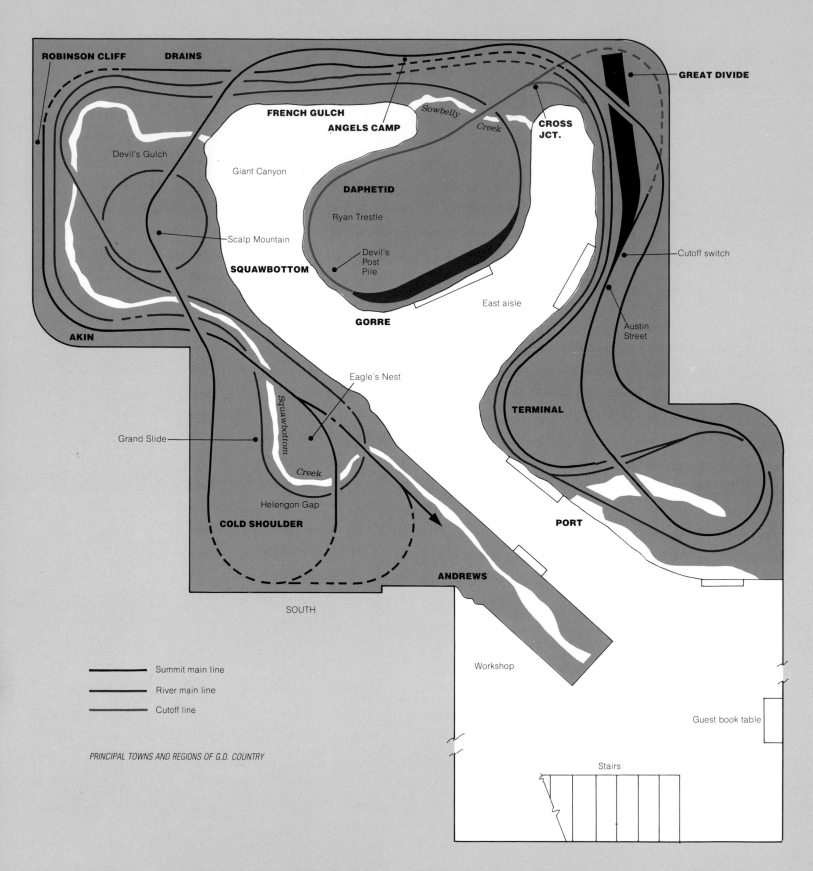

ROBINSON CLIFF   **DRAINS**

Devil's Gulch

FRENCH GULCH

ANGELS CAMP

Sowbelly

Creek

GREAT DIVIDE

Giant Canyon

DAPHETID

CROSS JCT.

Ryan Trestle

Scalp Mountain

Devil's Post Pile

Cutoff switch

SQUAWBOTTOM

East aisle

GORRE

Austin Street

AKIN

Eagle's Nest

TERMINAL

Grand Slide

Squawbottom

Creek

Helengon Gap

PORT

COLD SHOULDER

ANDREWS

SOUTH

Workshop

———— Summit main line

———— River main line

———— Cutoff line

Guest book table

PRINCIPAL TOWNS AND REGIONS OF G.D. COUNTRY

Stairs

odd mix of business, hotels, industry, cafes, gas works, packing plants, and harbor facilities.

Continuing toward Gorre, the line passes through more mountains, this time nearer to the bottoms of the canyons. The lowest point is along Squawbottom Creek at the Squaw-bottom station. From there a final grade lifts the line into Gorre, the far terminal of the railroad. Now John continues his narrative: "Out of Gorre a standard gauge branch runs north to Daphetid. Gorre is also a terminal for the D.G.& H. narrow gauge feeder being built to Helengon."

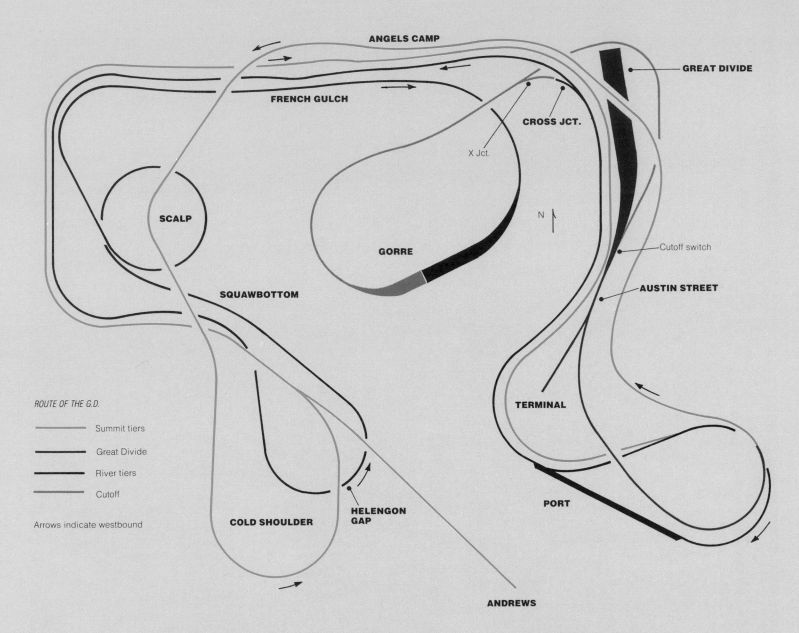

ANGELS CAMP

GREAT DIVIDE

FRENCH GULCH

CROSS JCT.

X Jct.

SCALP

N

GORRE

Cutoff switch

SQUAWBOTTOM

AUSTIN STREET

ROUTE OF THE G.D.

Summit tiers

Great Divide

River tiers

Cutoff

TERMINAL

Arrows indicate westbound

COLD SHOULDER

HELENGON GAP

PORT

ANDREWS

"Due to the ruggedness of the mountain passes and necessary 4 percent compensated ruling grades the railroad has many operating and economic problems. Operationwise we are concerned with moving through-train tonnage over the mountains and handling pickup and delivery freight for this division from our classification yard in Great Divide. Locos are not large due to the sharp curves and light rail, so tonnages must be considered carefully for the 4 percent grades. Although we do sometimes handle long trains with two or three locos, this is not our common practice due to the relatively short passing sidings. Speeds are fairly low.

"The G.D. is not 'big time,' though it is Class 1. Operation is more like that of the 1920s than the '40s. There is neither CTC nor block signaling. All operation is regulated by time schedule and train orders. Train orders are usually oral rather than written and are used principally when we are

This train is emerging from the Cutoff route track just east of Great Divide passenger terminal. Examine the photo closely and you'll spot at least eight of the hundreds of figures that populate the layout.

Port station is the building with the pyramid roof on its tower near the center of this photo.
From below it come the return loop track and the upper tier main line. The car ferry Anabel
is in the shipping basin, just about ready to tie up in her ferry slip.

occasionally forced to supersede the regular time schedules.

"After the last bridge is installed, the main line will be 6.7 scale miles or a little over 400 feet long. The railroad was planned for small group operation rather than for display. Weekly operation takes place with seven regular operators. There is no club organization though most of us travel to the NMRA region and division conventions together.

"Except for the locomotives, half the cars, and a few structures, all models on the G.D. are homebuilt. This includes the bridges, scenery, roadbed, track, many human figures, and some of the automobiles. I don't build instead of buying to save money. I enjoy the headwork of planning and the challenge of constructing what I have planned.

"For some reason visitors often ask how much the railroad cost; this seems to be especially interesting to the wives. I've never kept books on time or money spent on the railroad just as I don't on the books that I have read or movies attended. However, I did make a calculation based upon adding up and estimating and found it to be equivalent to the cost of two packs of cigarettes a day."

John doesn't smoke and he never allows smoking in the railroad room because it would alter the coloring of the scenery and affect the pickup of electrical power from the rails. His visitors are always welcome to return upstairs for a smoke.

The route through the mountains. —— The mainline route on the G.D. track plan is not immediately apparent. One problem with learning it is that the present route is not the same as the eventual one because some track isn't installed yet. I'll explain the official route first, then outline how only part of it is used as main line at present.

To be able to fit his concept into the railroad room, John folded the main line over itself in four tiers. It is easier to understand once you know that the Great Divide yard is at a fairly high elevation. From there the main line climbs over the highest elevation at Angels Camp and then zigzags downgrade along the walls, first counterclockwise, then clockwise, then over again. Each transit is made on the next lower tier until the bottom sag is reached. From there a brief climb

(Above) This is the panorama every G.D. visitor sees as he comes down the stairs and turns to his left toward the railroad. The sprawling city of Port is to the right of center, in the foreground, Great Divide engine terminal is just to the left, and Giant Canyon is at extreme left. East Port (below) features half a dozen industrial sidings, barge traffic, the East Port yard office, and the towering Port Plastics manufacturing complex. Below Port Plastics, at the lower right corner of the photo, is John's Subway gag, where the "train" rumbles ominously but never arrives.

Because the climate here is relatively mild year 'round, most of the servicing tracks at the Great Divide engine terminal are located outdoors. Snowplows, maintenance-of-way cars, and other non-revenue cars are also stored in this area.

Scenery extends all the way to the floor in magnificent Giant Canyon. Here, tier upon tier of climbing, twisting main line captures the flavor of railroading in rugged mountain country. The log train on the left is on Sims Loop, while the old-time train in the distance is actually a reflection in a mirror of a train near Akin.

takes the track to the lower terminal of the division at Gorre.

In the diagram on page 10, the top two tiers are shown as the "Summit" subdivision and the lower two layers are the "River" subdivision. These are so labeled only for your convenience; the operators do not distinguish between these subdivisions yet, because the last, or "Great" bridge is still to be installed between Scalp Mountain, left center, and Angels Camp, on the top tier. Without this bridge, only the lower two tiers, the River subdivision, are used as main line. The unconnected stubs of what are labeled the Summit subdivision are treated as separate branch lines.

The unfinished bridge also explains why the actual route of a mainline train on the G.D., which we will follow in the next chapter, is not the same as the route John described for us. Unfortunately, the missing bridge isolates the principal yard and terminal at Great Divide from the rest of the railroad. To get past this obstacle to smooth operation John has provided a sneak connection. To use it, trains leaving Great Divide back out of the yard and station area to the track opposite the Austin Street suburban station. From here they move forward and down the track indicated as the "Cutoff." They

soon reach Gorre, via a "back door" through Cross Junction.

This changes the order in which trains reach the stations and so makes Gorre, for the present, a way station instead of the distant terminus. Port now serves as the temporary distant terminus. All of this is likely to be confusing until you trace the routes with your finger on the track plan.

The view from Port. —— Let's go down to see the railroad. John descends the narrow stairway ahead of us to turn on the lights. (The basement window is covered so daylight does not interfere with the model railroad lighting.) Beyond the bottom step is a small table where everyone signs the guest book.

On your first visit to the G.D. Line you might not notice the workshop. You pass by it as you turn left from the foot of the stairs. What catches your attention is the colorful scene ahead. It is the city of Port, which fills an alcove in the southeast corner of the railroad room.

Port represents a harbor situated on a river and surrounded by railroad tracks and industrial buildings. In the harbor, the car ferry *Anabel* is loading freight cars. Beyond

Headquarters for this division of the railroad are located in the tall office building above the great arched portal of Great Divide passenger terminal. The apparent size of the modest classification yard here is doubled by the mirror positioned behind it.

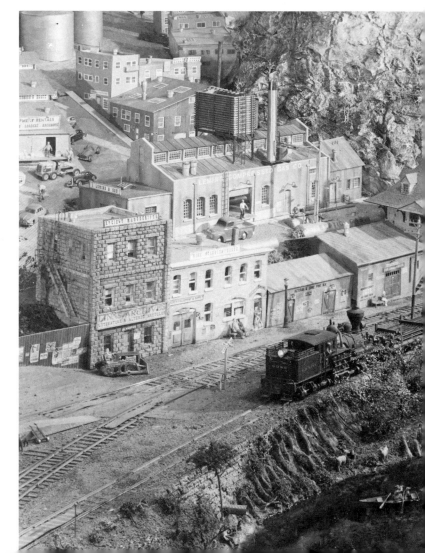

Bustling West Divide, located between the Great Divide engine terminal and the passenger yard, is the site of the control panel for the yard. The station is also served by the Cooper Electric trolley line.

The town of Andrews, tucked in the mountain highlands south of Helengon Gap, is a former resort that has gradually been taken over by heavy industry and agricultural business.

the waterfront, other cars are switched into sidings between factories. There are 18 individual industries on the railroad in Port. High above, another railroad line spans the harbor diagonally on a humped "Pennsylvania" Pratt truss bridge.

Port is 43 inches above the basement floor, and fills an area roughly 9 feet long and 7 feet deep. At your right and at the rear there is a sky backdrop, and the sky is filled with smoke from all the local industries. You hear the noise of a subway train low to your right. You can see the track and waiting commuters through an opening in the quay wall below the street. Guests have stood here, nearly hypnotized, for several minutes waiting to see the subway cars appear. It is one of John's practical jokes that the ever-rumbling train never arrives. A hidden tape recorder plays the subway noises continuously. Actually less than a foot of subway track is modeled, but through the use of mirrors the subway tunnel seems to bend far around a curve.

Scale versus distance.
—— All of the G.D. track, cars, and foreground scenery is modeled to HO scale, which makes a human figure stand just under an inch tall. All HO models are 1/87 of full size, but to create the illusion of greater distances, some of John's modeling beyond the railroad trackage is still smaller in scale. The transition is gradual and not easily detected.

Some modelers venerate the scale they use almost religiously, even to the point of disliking fine models in other sizes. John practices no such reverence toward his choice of HO scale: "I'm one of the oddballs who has no favorite scale or gauge. Each seems to have certain advantages and disadvantages, but I'd just as soon visit a layout built in a scale other than the one I work with. It is the ingenuity, effort, and care that the modeler puts in that catches my interest most." John adds that ever since mass production of railroad models in HO scale became a reality, many layouts have tended to have the same features. In such cases he'd rather see a layout of some other scale.

Now look to the left of Port and take in the sweeping panorama of G.D. territory. The distant half of the room is entirely mountains. Some peaks touch the ceiling while their steep slopes fall to the floor on each side of the aisleway. Here the walking surface represents a river flowing through a gorge called "Giant Canyon."

The room is nearly rectangular, but has alcoves in two of the walls. Overall it measures 23 x 32 feet. The main aisleway, which is 3 feet wide with irregular boundaries, runs diagonally to the opposite or northwest corner, about 40 feet away. The distance appears much greater, partly due to the reduced scale of the trees on distant slopes and partly due to a disguised mirror in the far corner that reflects the mountain scenery and visually expands the room.

Beyond the middle of the room, Giant Canyon (the aisle) bends to the right and disappears behind a cone-shaped mountain called the Devils Post Pile, which touches the ceiling. The massive red rock Post Pile actually conceals a support column.

In all, three peaks dominate the mountain area of the layout. Devils Post Pile is in the center of the room. South of it is Eagle's Nest Peak, which also reaches the ceiling to conceal a support column. West of Devils Post Pile is Scalp Mountain, not quite as high. Scalp is distinctive in having a loop of railroad track spiraling completely around it. There was once a

support column here, too, but John removed it before building the railroad. He felt it was not needed under that part of the upper floor.

Colorful and quiet.
—— Although the room itself seems dark, all of the railroad and scenery is well lighted from fixtures hidden behind valances and shields that hang a few inches from the ceiling. This light-against-dark contrast makes colors seem all the more brilliant. The distant skies are blue while clouds seem to hover over pine-dotted crags of bisque-gray rock.

The room is quiet. John, usually a virtual word fountain, becomes miraculously silent in the railroad room. When entertaining visitors downstairs, he waits for them to begin any conversation. One of the regular G.D. operators, Joe Cain, explains: "John never volunteers to point features out to you on his layout. If you see something and ask about it, then he will tell you all about it, but he never points it out to you."

When operating with his crew John encourages only what little talk is necessary to keep trains moving. "Seldom are visitors invited to attend our operations," he tells us. "I estimate the amount of work we can do is in inverse ratio to the amount of talk going on. I think it is improper to invite someone and then ignore him for a couple of hours while we are occupied. Unless a visitor understands and might be a prospect to join the group, he is given another night to come to visit."

We walk along the main aisle to the center of the room and find another aisle that branches to the right, to the northeast. These two aisles are sufficient for all normal viewing and operation. In places far from an aisle, John has provided removable access hatches where he can pop up to perform maintenance.

While everything west of you now is mountains, if you look back you will see that the eastern half of the room is entirely cityscape. The modeling represents different cities depending upon which track a train is on. The city of Great Divide's yard and passenger station is in the northeast corner along the side aisle. As John said upstairs, this is the main terminus of the system. Great Divide Terminal (the roundhouse and service facility) is close to us at the intersection of the aisles. (During operation the fellows know by context whether the yard, station, or engine terminal is meant when someone says "Great Divide." Sometimes John will simply say "terminal" when he means the Great Divide engine facilities, so I shall use that distinction here: "terminal" refers to Great Divide engine terminal; "yard" and "station" are the other Great Divide facilities.)

Austin Street, a part of Great Divide, is the area east of the engine terminal. The G.D. has a small station there. The Cooper Electric trolley line from Port parallels the railroad along Austin Street for a few blocks. Austin was known only as "West Divide" before the station building was installed here. There is another track on the viaduct high above Austin. For trains up there, the halt is listed as Cooper on the railroad's more recent track diagrams. Finally, Port, which you know about already, is at the southeast end of the city complex.

On your first visit, the sheer size and complexity of the Gorre & Daphetid is almost overwhelming. Let's take a brief intermission before we return to Great Divide to begin an inspection of this spectacular railroad through the Akinbaks.

"There is a drama about rugged mountain railroads as they twist and spiral back upon themselves over almost unsurmountable obstacles in order to conquer a mountain pass."

The main line through the Akinbaks

THERE IS a wide, curved-top control panel near Great Divide yard where John has switched on the power to run a train for us. We are about to get a lesson on some of John's ideas about visitors.

As John said upstairs, the G.D. is designed for "operation" and that assumes movements from one terminal to another, rather than trains running in circles. Such operation is often considered uninteresting for visitors to watch. The argument against it maintains that because timetable operation calls for frequent stops and stations on a model railroad are close together, the trains are stopped more often than they are moving.

John disagrees: "I don't leave trains out on the line ready to run for visitors. I prefer to make up a train with a switcher, pull a loco out of the terminal, and leave town in a prototype manner. Even the train runners seem to like seeing this done. They seem to be more interested in what is going on than in watching the train rolling through the countryside.

"I break the train up again at the end of the run while they are still here. Visitors don't get a chance to see such operations done on most model railroads, so I don't think they feel it is wasted time."

John is about to couple up a passenger train at Great Divide station and send it out over the line. It will go through a place called "Cross Junction" first, and then make its first important stop at Gorre. After that it will thread its way through the mountains for a considerable distance before terminating at Port. As I mentioned in Chapter 1, this is not the order of stations and the terminal that John mentioned when describing the concept of the G.D. Until a very important bridge near the first mountain summit is completed, trains must leave Great Divide by a sort of back door, the Cutoff Line, to reach the rest of the railroad. Also, until that bridge is finished, the disconnected parts of the Summit subdivision must be treated as separate branch lines extending out of Great Divide at this end of the main line and Port at the other.

Our local passenger train is standing at the platform in Great Divide station without its locomotive. It consists of a baggage car, an express refrigerator car, a steel combination coach-baggage car, and a short wood combination that will be switched out at Gorre to be taken up the branch line to Daphetid.

Until the whole main line is completed things work backward at Great Divide. The train is made up in this stub-end station so that the rear-end cars come out first. The road engine can't be coupled to its train until later, after a switcher has pulled the cars out of the station.

John moves the switcher and the road engine alternately. There is a switcher pocket hidden behind the Rosalies Cannery building on the elevated line above Port, and John runs a switcher from there around the curved viaduct above the harbor and toward the train waiting in the station. Then he selects a road engine from the roundhouse and backs it onto the turntable.

The engine is Ten-Wheeler number 49, which John assigns to mainline local service about as often as any other engine. It is a modified Varney "Casey Jones" locomotive, a model about 20 years old. The switcher is engine 12, a Model

Towering Scalp Mountain dwarfs a Gorre & Daphetid freight train drifting downgrade on the approach span to Sims Loop trestle. This is the tightest curve on the twisting G.D. main line.

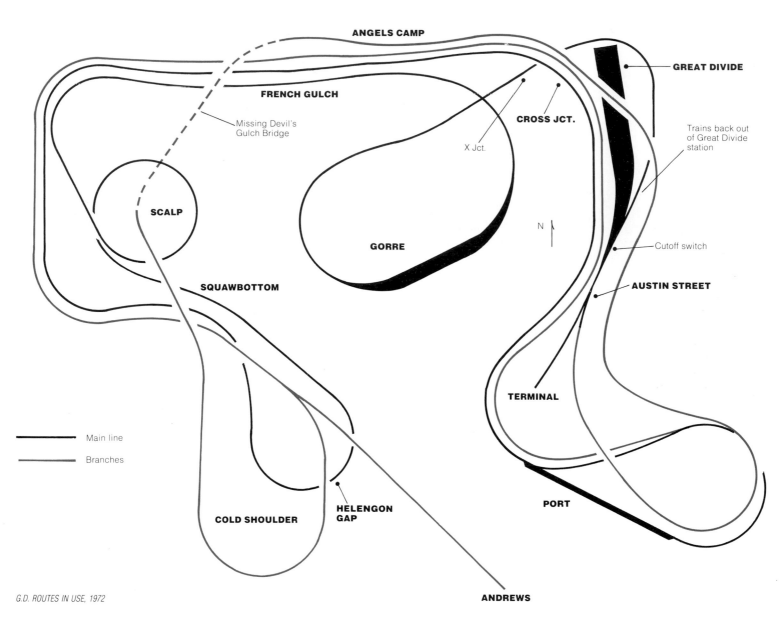

ANGELS CAMP

GREAT DIVIDE

FRENCH GULCH

Missing Devil's
Gulch Bridge

CROSS JCT.

X Jct.

Trains back out
of Great Divide
station

SCALP

N

GORRE

Cutoff switch

SQUAWBOTTOM

AUSTIN STREET

Main line

Branches

TERMINAL

COLD SHOULDER

HELENGON
GAP

PORT

G.D. ROUTES IN USE, 1972

ANDREWS

(Above) Looking east toward Cross Junction we see a train that has just left Great Divide emerging from the Cutoff track tunnel. For scheduling and operating purposes, any train on this track is said to be passing through or stopped at "X Junction."

(Right) You would have to rest your head on the floor near the end of Giant Canyon to see a train from this point of view. This is the G.D. Line's tallest wood trestle, over Ryan Gulch. Devils Post Pile, behind the locomotive, hides a floor-to-ceiling support column.

Die Casting 0-6-0. It couples onto the cars in the station and waits there.

After turning, road engine 49 rolls off the turntable, headed forward. It stops for water on the service track. At departure time the switcher pulls the train out of the station and uncouples from it at the Austin Street suburban platform. This move makes space for the road engine to pull ahead into Great Divide yard and then back onto the train.

John explains that while switching movements are made from local control panels, now he must move over to the main control panel at Gorre, north of the aisle intersection, to handle the train over the road. After the road engine couples onto the cars, the brakes are tested and the train departs. (Model trains don't really have brakes, but John pulls the train ahead just a little, then stops, to make sure all couplers are connected. This is called a brake test.)

On the first part of its journey, this train will start

(Left) Trains leaving Great Divide back out of the yard, then veer to the right into this tunnel and onto the "Cutoff" track. The train will then pass under the passenger terminal and emerge at Cross Junction.

headed north and then gradually turn counterclockwise toward the center of the room. By the time it gets partway along the line to Gorre it will have made almost a full 360-degree revolution, passing under, over, around, and through various parts of the scenery.

The Cutoff, and Cross Junction. —— Instead of going straight ahead into Great Divide station, engine 49 takes a right hand switch and leads our train into a tunnel in the hillside behind Great Divide. John has no special name for this important switch, so we'll refer to it as the "Cutoff switch." The hidden Cutoff track curves to the right, then left, then down and under Great Divide station to emerge at Cross Junction.

As soon as the Cutoff line emerges from the tunnel at Cross Junction, it crosses another track at grade. The other track is part of the River subdivision main line which our train will reach near the end of its journey.

We must walk toward Cross Junction (at the end of this side aisle) and look to the left to see the train continue westward, crossing Sowbelly Creek on a truss bridge. "This is

open range country and cattle graze anywhere. The locomotives need cowcatchers," John once wrote.

Beyond the bridge the roadbed cuts high into the south slope of Sowbelly ravine. The train is headed across the neck of the peninsula of benchwork that supports Gorre.

Down in the ravine is another track, one which our train will traverse in a few more minutes. We can also see the grade for the narrow gauge Devil's Gulch & Helengon Railroad under construction. The creek itself, like the water back in Port, is simulated with clear plastic poured and hardened in place.

All engine and train movements on the G.D. are made smoothly and at scale speeds. (A typical train speed of 35 scale miles per hour for HO scale is only 7 inches per second.) To the untrained visitor this seems slow, but it improves operation, especially considering how short the distances are between stops. John explains: "Train speeds are necessarily

The first switch at the entrance to Gorre yard extends right into the short tunnel through Devils Post Pile. This eastbound train has just whistled to signal its impending arrival at Gorre station.

(Left) The town of Gorre, located above the main control panel, is the G.D.'s junction point with the narrow gauge Devil's Gulch & Helegon. Halfway up the sloping terrain from Gorre, in the middle of this photo, is Daphetid, the railroad's other namesake town. Angels Camp, upper right, is the highest point on the line. (Right) While a switcher adds cars to a mainline train, G.D. Shay number 7 moves a log train across the straining beam truss bridge on the branch line at Gorre. In the background is the Squaw Creek High Bridge.

slow on a mountain line, but this has added advantages of increasing the apparent length of a model railroad. Time, rather than distances between stations, is the important operating factor."

Many model railroaders operate this way today, but John did it years ago when few model trains could perform smoothly or run slowly and even fewer model railroaders thought of scale speeds.

Since the train is not speeding, you have time to step around to the other aisle to see the scenery the train passes through over there. That aisle, you recall, is Giant Canyon, where the cliffs reach up from the floor.

The track bends south and crosses Ryan Gulch on a high timber trestle, the G.D.'s tallest. Immediately afterward, the train plunges into a short tunnel through the flank of Devils

Post Pile. The namesake town of Gorre is the next station.

Gorre. ——— To see the train arrive, walk back to the intersection of the aisles and face north. Gorre is directly in front of you above the mainline control panel. The train approaches from your left and slows to a smooth stop.

Gorre, although only a tiny village, has a few industries and is important to the railroad as the junction for both the short branch line to Daphetid and the narrow gauge Devil's Gulch & Helengon. The G.D. main line and its passing tracks are in front. Behind them is a small yard including some narrow gauge track, a tiny dual gauge turntable, and John's prizewinning two-stall enginehouse. We'll learn a bit more about it in Chapter 3. Next comes an elevated viaduct, partly masonry arches and partly timber truss bridge. The viaduct

The G.D.'s longest and highest span, the huge Scalp Mountain Arch, carries trains high above Squawbottom from Cold Shoulder (left) to Scalp Mountain. Trains on this bridge are fully five feet above the floor of John's basement.

(Right) The bridges at French Gulch are among the G.D.'s most famous features, and John's favorite photo setting. This train, on the lowest tier, is leaving Sowbelly, bound for Squawbottom. This is the only place where all four mainline tiers run parallel to one another, stacked against the wall.

(Below) "Drains" is the area west of French Gulch. The unfinished girder bridge section extending from the highest tier of track is the approach span for the great Devil's Gulch Bridge, the one that John never completed.

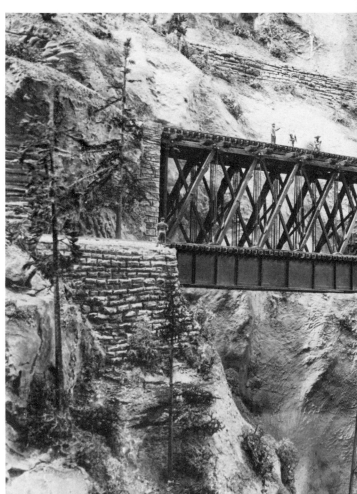

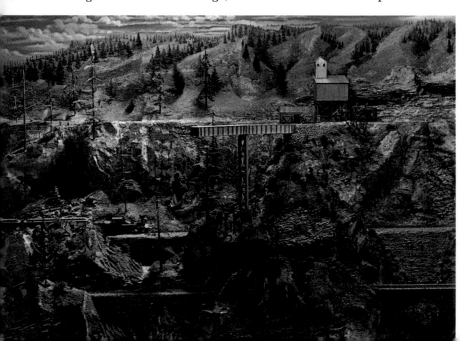

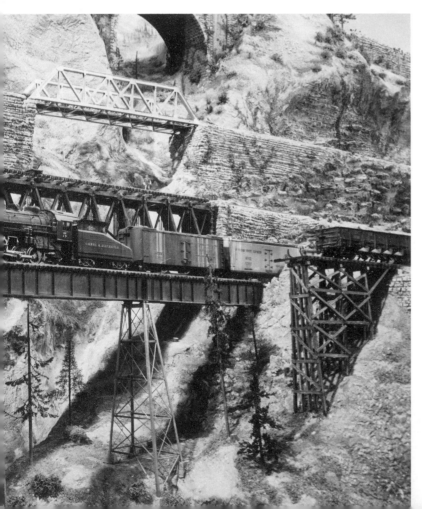

(Above) Devil's Gulch is a favorite haunt of fishermen, who reel tasty rainbow trout from a few placid pools along Squawbottom Creek. Above Devil's Gulch is rugged Robinson Cliff, and higher yet are the remains of a forest destroyed by a careless cigarette smoker.

(Above left) As a train headed for Squawbottom leaves Gorre on the lower track, a bright red streamlined consist headed for Cross Junction crosses above it on the truss bridge at Sowbelly.

supports part of the G.D.'s Daphetid branch. That line has 5 percent grades and 14-inch radius curves.

The Butler Mine, "where they get the lead out," John says, is half hidden behind the Devils Post Pile at the left end of the viaduct. Beyond the viaduct is tiny Taylor Lake, and above the lake is the hamlet of Daphetid. At the right are a few industries arrayed along a spur track.

If this part of the layout looks slightly different from the rest of the G.D., it is because the middle of this peninsula of benchwork, including Daphetid and half of Gorre, is actually John's very first model railroad, built in 1946. This original layout, only 3'-7" wide by 6'-8" long, is the tiny seed from which the present G.D. grew. The original G.D. was a two-lap oval, but when the layout was moved here, John abandoned part of the track to leave a branch line that traverses two switchbacks. Just below Daphetid you can see the weed-grown roadbed and an abandoned tunnel portal, remnants of the original line no longer used.

Shay-geared locomotive number 7 is switching at Gorre today. It pulls the short wood combine from the rear of our

Few visitors get to see this graceful concrete viaduct deep in Devil's Gulch behind Scalp Mountain. The passenger train on the viaduct is descending toward Squawbottom, while the double-headed freight behind is struggling up the 3.5 percent grade toward Port. High above and to the left is the tiny mountain town of Akin.

(Above) The constant rain-like mist from the waterfall at the headwaters of Squawbottom Creek results in lush vegetation in this corner of wild Helengon Gap. The lower track here is the G.D. main eastbound out of Squawbottom, and the curved-chord Warren deck truss bridge carrying the train above it is on the Andrews branch south of Eagle's Nest.

train, backs into Post Pile tunnel, then moves forward into Gorre yard. Soon the combine will be sent up the branch line to Daphetid.

While our mainline train is standing still, let's look around the room.

Bridges. —— Bridges, bridges, bridges; John says he once counted 130 of them. They are everywhere, yet every one is needed to support the railroad over a street, stream, chasm, or other track. "I enjoy the study of bridges," John answers to a question. "Probably one of the principal reasons I chose a mountain railroad is that so many bridges are required, even though they take much time to construct."

John scratchbuilt most of the G.D. Line bridges, including all of the large ones. He used cardboard, wood, styrene, and occasionally brass. In several instances he has carved linoleum to represent stonework. John varied the design of the bridges as though they were built by several companies and at various times.

Across the aisle and to the left from where you stand at Gorre you see the four largest bridges on the G.D. Line.

Three of them radiate from Eagle's Nest Peak. Closest to you is a Warren deck truss with curved bottom chords spanning Helengon Gap. Look farther into Helengon Gap and you see a steel arch bridge supporting another track. The tracks from these two Helengon bridges flank the opposite sides of Eagle's Nest Peak to join each other just west of the peak. The joined line continues across a straight Warren deck truss on tall concrete piers. This is Squaw Creek High Bridge. Until recently it was the highest bridge on the railroad, 192 scale feet above the stream.

Today, in 1972, there is a still higher bridge, the Scalp Mountain Arch Bridge, which supports part of the top tier of the G.D.'s unfinished Summit subdivision main line. It crosses Squawbottom Creek just west of the High Bridge and reaches the railroad's summit on top of Scalp Mountain. Here the track is 60 inches above the floor and 30 inches above the railroad's low point, which is directly below the bridge at Squawbottom station. In HO scale terms, Scalp Mountain Arch is 407 feet long and carries the future main line 220 feet above Squawbottom Creek.

We will get down to Squawbottom presently, but there is

(Left) Two G.D. trains meet at Squawbottom siding, deep in the canyon along Squawbottom Creek. The massive Scalp Mountain Arch Bridge had not been built when this photo was taken, otherwise it would dominate the upper right-hand portion of the picture.

crossed over before reaching Gorre. Since a log pond and an active lumber camp are located along the stream, the train makes a brief stop at Sowbelly station to let off some loggers who had spent their weekend in the city. Logs are cut upstream and dropped into the creek where they float down to a pile dam. There they are hoisted onto cars for the trip to the sawmills at Andrews, a town on one of the branch lines. Sowbelly also has an oil well. Beside the side track are a few tanks where crude oil is held for loading into tank cars.

French Gulch. —— Now the train comes to perhaps the best-known scenic feature on the G.D. Line, French Gulch. Here, a steep gully cuts diagonally down through an even steeper cliff of rock. All four tiers of the railroad must cross the gully, each on a different type of bridge. This is John's favorite location for photographing G.D. rolling stock.

The lowest tier, where our train is now, has a modern three-span steel girder trestle on a new alignment. You can see the remnants of the previous timber trestle at the Sowbelly end. The bridge on the next higher tier was built jointly by the narrow gauge and standard gauge railroads, for they share three-rail track on that tier. Because it was financed by both railroads, an expensive, solidly built timber truss design was used here. It is one of the oldest bridges on the line.

The third span across French Gulch is a short through pony truss span that our train will traverse just before reaching Cross Junction. The uppermost tier crosses the gulch on a handsome masonry arch. This arch is on the stub-end branch at Angels Camp, but when the last great bridge over Devil's Gulch is complete, the masonry arch will carry the main line toward the summit at Scalp Mountain.

Many more ravines cut through these cliffs, and at every ravine each tier of track requires a bridge, or at the very minimum, a retaining wall with a drain. Because of this, the next area west of French Gulch is known as "Drains."

You may recall that you are standing on the "water" of Giant Canyon. If you pivot full left to look past Drains and up Devil's Gulch, you'll see a large canyon leading west, then bending south. Its bottom rises, first suddenly, then more gradually from floor elevation. The missing great Devil's Gulch Bridge will complete the main line by spanning Devil's Gulch close to where you now stand. This huge bridge will take the top tier of railroad from above Drains to the top of Scalp Mountain to join the present end of track.

The western wall of rock facing you where Devil's Gulch turns is Robinson Cliff. It has the scars of a forest fire upon its upper reaches. High to the right and far away you see the village of Nika. Nika doesn't really exist. It is the mirror image in both sight and spelling of Akin, a village actually modeled in the southwest corner of the railroad room. The same mirror that made the room look larger from the entrance reflects Nika here. Clouds painted on the sky overlap this seven-foot-wide mirror to disguise its edges. The overall effect is stunning.

While the creek in Devil's Gulch can be walked upon,

something I should mention before we arrive there. Visitors, and even G.D. operators, find the names Squawbottom and Sowbelly are easily confused. It might help to forget how sows are built and remember that for people, at least, the bottom is on a lower tier than the belly.

Back at Gorre our passenger train is ready to pull out. This time it will make another great turn counterclockwise against the north and west walls of the room, followed by a tighter loop around Scalp Mountain. It will wind down to Squawbottom headed southeast, having turned almost three counterclockwise circles since leaving Great Divide. Beyond Squawbottom the line climbs more than a full circle in the opposite direction to reach the present terminal at Port.

The "brake test" has been made to check the couplers and the passenger train starts out of Gorre. From there to Squawbottom the ruling grade is 4 percent down, steep enough to keep the brakes smoking. Instead of following the train, we walk the other way into Giant Canyon to get a good view of the train coming around the hill into Sowbelly Ravine.

The train soon appears, rolling under the bridge it had

This view looking south from Squawbottom shows the G.D. main line winding out of Helengon Gap, past Grand Slide, and along Squawbottom Creek. High above is remote and snowy Cold Shoulder, made doubly distant by the mirror near the center of this photo.

John never invites visitors to go in there because the bridges and scenic features on the mountainsides are especially fragile. If you could sneak up there, you would discover that the valley bends around Scalp Mountain in a "U" shape. At the other end of the "U" is Squaw Valley and its big bridges.

Rather than fully excavate this part of the basement to floor level, John shaped an irregular bend of natural earth through Devil's Gulch and Squaw Valley. He covered the earth with a three-inch layer of concrete to surface the gulch. This made the creek bottom waterproof, and strong enough to walk upon for maintenance.

Real water can be fed to the outlet of the log pond at Andrews in the far southeast corner of the room. The water then tumbles down a waterfall in Helengon Gap, follows concreted Squaw Valley around the back side of both Eagle's Nest Peak and Scalp Mountain, and cascades, finally, from Devil's Gulch into Giant Canyon just below Drains. A floor drain in the aisle keeps the water from flooding the basement.

Our train follows these U-shaped valleys, disappearing for a moment behind Scalp Mountain. Then it makes a complete counterclockwise circuit of Scalp Mountain on a descending helical spiral called Sims Loop.

The front side of Scalp Mountain is known as Grandt Cliff. Here the railroad seems high above Giant Canyon, but

John points out that it is actually near the lowest part of G.D. trackage. One of John's favorite photographic tricks is to stop a train on the loop's steel trestle, lay a mirror on the aisle floor, and aim the camera down into the mirror for a striking upward view of the train.

Squawbottom. —— Once around the mountain again and our train reaches Squawbottom, where a freight train is waiting on the passing track for our passenger consist to clear the switch. The station at Squawbottom is one of my favorite structures on the Gorre & Daphetid system. John and his friend Jim Findley spent quite a little time building it, a story we'll return to.

North of the station on a spur track is another masterpiece of structure modeling, the Cinnabar Mine. Jim Findley made the Cinnabar Mine for his own Tioga Pass railroad, but installed it on the G.D. instead. John made the mechanical tip car mechanism and installed it. Jim also made a number of other G.D. structures, including the gasholder in Port, the stations at Cross Junction and Daphetid, and the "hunting lodge" (employees' bunkhouse) here at Squawbottom.

After a brief station stop our train departs Squawbottom. For a short distance along the creek the railroad is a water level route, but very soon the track begins to climb a 3.5

The two-level station at busy Cross Junction is one of the Gorre & Daphetid's most distinctive buildings. The cutoff line emerges from the tunnel at lower left, and the upper level stop, where gas-electric car number 60 is loading passengers, is called Corsa.

percent compensated grade. The track skirts the base of Eagle's Nest Peak, then bends into dark and wild Helengon Gap. There the train loops around the base of the peak to hairpin back the other way, now gaining elevation above Squawbottom Creek. This is the beginning of the next higher tier of mountainside running.

On this tier, the train follows along the south, west, and north walls of the room on the next tier above the bottom. As the train glides across French Gulch on the timber truss and approaches a fairly long tunnel, it whistles for Cross Junction just beyond the tunnel. All trains on this track must whistle and make a safety stop before entering Cross Junction. Pushbuttons at each control panel operate the same motor-blown whistle under the bench for all trains.

Cross Junction has perhaps the most interesting station on the system. It is a three-story building with passenger platforms on two track levels. An outdoor stairway connects them. When asked about it, John tells us pretty much what he had said in the May 1968 MODEL RAILROADER:

"On the G.D. Line, local passenger and mail trains stop here on both levels. Bilevel stations have much value on model railroads, where tracks looping over and under each other are common. They allow you two station features while cluttering the layout with only one structure. Two-level stations exist on the prototype, but I doubt if any had different names for the two elevations." (Our train up from Squawbottom is at "Cross Junction," but a train on the upper level would be at "Corsa.")

Squawbottom Mine is located inside the spiral at Sims Loop, but is reached by a spur from near the station at Squawbottom. John's friend Jim Findley built the model, a cinnabar mine.

As eastbound G.D. trains emerge from the alcove behind Eagle's Nest they pass through this short rock tunnel just above Squawbottom siding. The grade from here to Port is a demanding 3.5 percent.

"While I took the part of the architect," John continues, "the station itself is Jim Findley's fine construction. The actual area this building covers is only eight square inches. By designing three levels and using a large visible roof area the station gains the appearance of a larger building."

In all, four routes pass the station at Cross Junction and Corsa. The first is the Cutoff, the route our train took shortly after leaving Great Divide. On this route the place is officially labeled "X Junction" (although operators usually call it "Cross Junction" regardless).

The second route is the second tier of the main line, the River subdivision route over which our train has just come. It crosses the Cutoff at grade. As John told us, Cross Junction is the official name on this route. A wye track connects these two routes, making a third routing.

The main line, third tier, passes through the upper level of the station. This is the lower tier of the Summit subdivision. This track is reached by a stairway to the upper platform, and up here the station is called Corsa.

Both the River and Summit main lines from Cross Junction and Corsa to the right of the station lead directly to Port, hanging on the front edge of the benchwork past Great Divide and the Terminal. These tracks have no switches or scenic features to distract the eye from the more interesting yards and enginehouse behind them.

One of John's regular operators has been switching cars at Port and John pushes the whistle button to warn him that our passenger train is about to arrive. Then, until given a green signal by the yard operator, John must hold his train outside the yard limit.

The facilities at Port, never intended as a terminus, are so cramped that it takes an experienced operator to keep up with the work here. Switching has to be done using the main line as a lead. There is storage room for only two or three short trains, and then only if Port is not clogged with cars to be sorted. If a train stands on the main line waiting to get in, thus blocking the line so another train cannot get out, the whole railroad can come to a standstill.

There is a signal on Railroad Avenue that can be seen from the mainline panel at Gorre. The Port operator tells the

Trains reaching Port from Squawbottom, as is the case here, take the right-hand route into the balloon loop, cross the mouth of the harbor, and enter Port station, the gray building with the peaked tower, from right to left. Here the car ferry Anabel is in the slip and the always-busy Port switcher is sorting cars for her next departure.

road engineers what he wants by changing the color of this signal from his yard panel. Red means stop, green is come ahead, and yellow means back up. We have the green so John runs the train in.

The track makes a return loop around the harbor at Port, eliminating the need for space-consuming turntables and runaround pockets. The passenger station is the structure with a pyramid tower on the north side of the harbor. Normally trains reach it going counterclockwise through the loop.

Our train has finished its journey, having covered all of the River subdivision and the Cutoff line but none of the Summit subdivision. Andrews is the most important town on

that line, and is presently served by branchline trains out of Port. After an operating session, the gang usually goes upstairs for half an hour or more of chatting over coffee. As guests, we'll do the same.

John never told the operators much about his personal life and only a little about getting started in model railroading. But from bits he told this fellow and that, and me, and with the help of his brother Andrew and his letters to other modelers, I have pieced together the stories of John's early life and how the first Gorre & Daphetid came to be built. Those subjects fill the next chapter. Later on, we'll learn how the layout we've just examined was planned and constructed, how it operated, and, sadly, how it was destroyed.

GORRE & DAPHETID R.R.

"A model railroad should probably start with a concept, but seldom will a first model railroad have one. Why? Because much knowledge about railroading, experience in model railroading, and thought are required before a proper concept for a model railroad can be formed. These requirements are seldom possible on a first pike. Mine was no exception."

The first
Gorre & Daphetid

IN A SENSE, John Allen began in September 1946 to build the large Gorre & Daphetid layout we have just visited in 1972. The story of the construction of this layout spans more than a quarter century, and includes such diverse activities as building locomotives and cars, attending National Model Railroad Association meets, constructing the layout, arguing a fine point of operation with a friend, pontificating in a wide-ranging model railroad bull session, or playing a practical joke. Before beginning to weave these hundred and one themes and details together, let me outline briefly the five principal stages of the Gorre & Daphetid.

Five stages of the G.D. —— Stage 1: John began railroad modeling in 1944. He first built two freight cars, several structures, fences, windmills, baggage trucks, and a number of miniature animals and human figures. His first published magazine article, in 1946, showed the models arranged realistically on a tabletop, and told how to photograph such displays.

Stage 2: In 1946 and 1947 John constructed a very small

John scratchbuilt "old G.D." number 2, the C.D. Grandt, and photographed it leaving the tunnel portal just below Daphetid on the first G.D. In order to pull a train, this tiny dummy locomotive required a "helper" in the form of a powered old-time gondola car.

rectangular layout. This original Gorre & Daphetid was about the size of a wide door panel. It was portable, and rested on a dining table. Late in 1947 he began constructing his two-stall enginehouse, the model that first attracted the attention of many other railroad modelers.

Stage 3: During 1948 John refined the portable layout and built more cars and an old-time 4-2-0 engine. Then John became interested in narrow gauge. For this he first built some HOn3 cars, and then constructed Mount Alexander and the village of Helengon, a small yard across the aisle from his main layout. Later this Devil's Gulch & Helengon Railroad was connected to the main layout by a lift-out bridge section. Narrow gauge track was extended gradually, reaching Gorre by 1952.

Stage 4: The layout became permanent late in 1948, and plans were drawn to fill a space measuring 6 feet 6 inches by 20 feet 6 inches. The first extension, in December, included the Great Divide terminal along the rear wall and a set of end curves for a new, twice-around main line.

From 1949 until 1953 John built most of the track and scenery for this expanded G.D. layout, and added many new cars and locomotives to the G.D. roster.

Stage 5: The culmination of John's efforts was the large G.D. layout at Cielo Vista Terrace. It was begun in 1954. Track and scenery were all new except that the original door-

These very early photos from John's "tabletop period" show most of his early modeling projects. The structures were scratchbuilt from cardstock and wood, as were several of the cars. When these and other photos appeared in the model railroad magazines, many readers were astonished by the lifelike lighting, background, and details.

size G.D. was saved, modified, and included as part of the new railroad. All of the old structures and rolling stock were also saved. Construction of this final G.D. continued with only minor interruptions until John's death in 1973.

John's family background had a lot to do with his having the time to build so much so well, so let's talk about it.

Aunts, uncles, grandparents, and brothers. —— John Whitby Allen, the third son of Austin Allen, a prominent architect, was born on July 2, 1913, in Joplin, Missouri. Three years later his father contracted typhoid fever during a hunting trip in Florida, and died at age 35. John's older brother, Andrew Allen, told me of John's early life:

"Mother was quite young, three or four years younger than my father. It was quite a blow to her. She took me East with her and left the other two boys with our grandmother. Then shortly after that she took us out to California. We lived in Pasadena, Los Angeles, and then San Diego, where we had relatives. Then they caught the flu (during the World War I epidemic) so we went across the bay to Coronado. When mother also became ill she put us in a school on Point Loma [San Diego].

"Mother died when we were in that school. I was about 9 and Jack [John was called "Jack" as a young man] would have been 6. We went back to Missouri at the end of that school year."

The grandparents on both sides of the family lived in Joplin. The eldest brother, Austin, stayed with the paternal grandmother, Andrew stayed with the maternal grandmother, and Jack was sent to live with his Aunt Mie.

A broken family is difficult for any growing person, and so is moving, but John once told my wife, Harriet, that although he was moved from one relative and place to another, he was thankful that he and his brothers were always cared for by loving relatives.

After grammar school, the boys were sent to Shattuck Military Academy in Faribault, Minnesota. Jack went to Junior School first—for upper grade school students—then he went to Shattuck itself, high school level, but only for one year.

He did not like the regimentation in the lower school:

"He disliked it so much," Andrew said. "They had this system of punishment: if you didn't work in your garden, they would first give you castor oil. And if that didn't work, they would hold your head under the shower. Jack was willing to take those punishments and he still wasn't going to work in the garden. He'd come back to the garden and sit on the ground and play a race between snails. He could find all kinds of things to do but he just refused to work for them.

"Well then, when he got to the military school, he had to get up at 5:45 in the morning, make his bed, do his sitting up exercises—it was pretty cold there in the winter in Minnesota—and he objected to that. I objected to it, too, but not as much as he did.

"At that time, Jack caught rheumatic fever. On the doctor's advice he moved to California. Aunt Mie and her husband had moved out there by that time. He lived with them part of the time, then went off on his own in a rooming house."

John's health improved as a result of his move to California, but his bout with rheumatic fever weakened his heart and eventually led to his death at age 59.

Shattuck Academy was not the end of Jack's military experiences. After he finished high school, he attended UCLA, and there he joined the ROTC. He liked that much more than his previous regimented experiences, and from then on he always felt at home with military personnel. This brought its reward years later when John enlisted the help of servicemen in Monterey to operate the Gorre & Daphetid.

Art training, and good fortune. —— In 1934, John and Andrew visited the Century of Progress World's Fair in Chicago. That exposition gave model railroading a fine start here in America because several railroad companies installed exhibits of scale model trains. These scale models were much more detailed than the toys people were used to seeing. John liked trains and most certainly was impressed.

At UCLA John majored in economics with the idea of a career in business. He got good grades, but the subject somehow didn't appeal to him. After two years he switched to art school, eventually specializing in photography. He attended art school for three years.

In this 1950 portrait by Glenn Beier, John posed hard at work laying new track behind the prizewinning Gorre enginehouse.

Art school provided some fine tools which John later used to advantage in model railroading. He mastered lighting, the human figure, perspective, color, illusions, lettering, the chemical properties of pigments, the use of brushes, and, of course, photography. After art school, John and another student named Waite set up a studio in the Westlake Park neighborhood of Los Angeles. They concentrated on commercial and advertising photography.

When John's paternal grandparents died, they had accumulated a modest amount of money. When the boys became of age, this inheritance was distributed, and in 1935 Andy and John each received about $1900. To put this into perspective, at the time, that amount was equal to about one year's income for a middle class family.

(Above) John achieved exceptional realism in his tabletop model railroad photos by simulating strong sunlight and bright sky, and by framing the subjects with strong artistic elements such as the tree limbs in this March 1946 photo.

John once again placed himself in the picture when he showed how he made and photographed his tabletop scenes in his first article for MODEL RAILROADER magazine. The framework for the first Gorre & Daphetid layout was already under construction, and in this photo it is resting on its edge at John's right.

Instead of buying a car or spending it in some other way, both invested their funds. This was one of the most important things John ever did, for it made him financially independent in 11 years. "From 1946 until the time he died," Andy relates, "John's stocks went up a great deal more. Long before he died he did not have to be concerned about money." By the time John died, his original inheritance had grown to over half a million dollars as a result of Andy's management of his investments and John's frugal living habits.

Andy comments on John's lifestyle:

"He was very analytical and he would pick out flaws in what society was doing and expose them; the fallacies of our ways of living such as having styles, dressing up all the time, showing off. Since I was in the investment and accounting world, where you have to follow tradition more than you might want to on your own, we didn't live the same, but I agreed with him in many ways that there is too much false front, too much display, buying new cars, having the latest styles of clothing, and so forth."

Monterey, and model railroading. —— John's interest in model railroading may have started to develop before World War II. Andy relates: "Before the war, in 1939, he and I would go up to San Francisco, occasionally, to see Aunt Lucille and her husband Morgan Taylor in Piedmont, near Oakland. Sometime before then Uncle Morgan had acquired a model railroad and Jack had the idea of working on it. Jack

John cut out the sign for his HO scale Owens-Parks Lumber Co. from a Los Angeles phone book, then sent a print of this photo to the firm, saying in jest that he liked their name so well he decided to use it on his own lumberyard. The Los Angeles firm responded by sending a Monterey lawyer to visit John concerning the infringement!

had made other types of models—airplanes, automobiles, and ships—so he took to it and enjoyed it."

The war came and with it, the draft of young men into service. The oldest brother, Austin, had been killed in an automobile accident in 1940. Andy went into the service and was stationed briefly in northern California. John knew that his heart condition would prevent him from being accepted for active duty, but he thought he might work in aerial photography interpretation. This way he would be serving but not regimented, and that appealed to him. John's friend Jim Findley quipped, "John liked regimentation—for someone else. He felt that his creative abilities would probably be put to use in the Army." He was disappointed when they would not take him even for such help.

While Andy was stationed in northern California, John visited him and discovered the attractive town of Monterey. He felt there would be photographic business due to the influx of military people, so he and a partner, Weston Booth, set up a studio in town on Alvarado, a main street, with a branch stand in the Presidio where they did a brisk business photographing servicemen.

"By 1946," Andy said, "when the war ended he had made

enough money so he could sell his photography business and invest that money in addition to what he already had. He could spend his time as he wished."

It was model railroading that interested him most.

Starting from scratch—no kits! —— John attributed his active start in model railroading to discovering a MODEL RAILROADER magazine and some scale models in an Oakland department store hobby shop in 1944. At that time there were only a score of hobby shops in all North America.

The hobby was not at all like it is today. Early manufactured products had been relatively crude and when the war started, production had stopped completely. Those who for one reason or another were not out of the country in military service made do with the few kits still unsold or built from raw materials.

Even before the war, finished models rarely had been offered. Nearly everything was parts or kits. Few parts were well detailed and the selection was not extensive.

In this situation, even if John had wanted to assemble models from kits, he couldn't have done much of it. Until the coming of imported brass locomotives, nearly all of his mod-

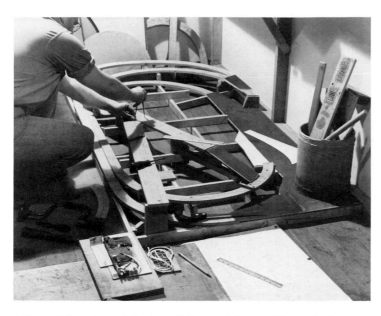

(Above) John planned the first G.D. carefully, and he made frequent reference both to a small model of the layout and a benchwork model as he built the railroad. The wide, straight roadbed section nearest the camera is the eventual site of Daphetid.

(Right) The train order signal and interior detail of the little Gorre station show up well in this dramatic night switching scene near the front edge of the layout.

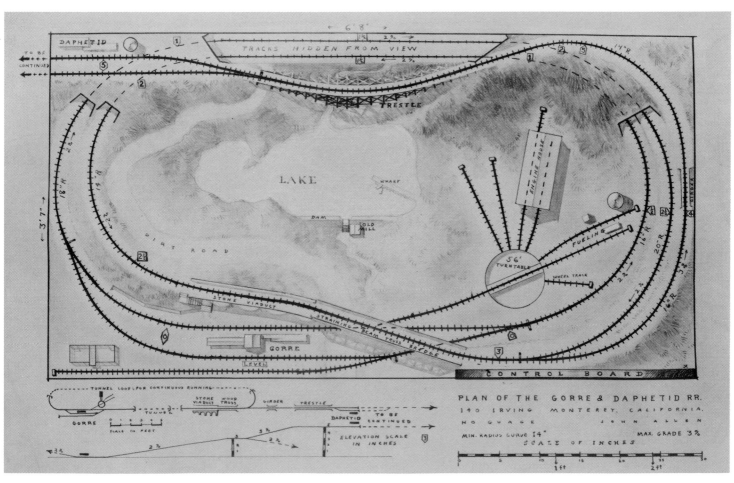

PLAN OF THE GORRE & DAPHETID RR.
140 IRVING MONTEREY, CALIFORNIA.
HO GUAGE   JOHN ALLEN
MIN. RADIUS CURVE 14"   MAX. GRADE 3%
SCALE OF INCHES

(Above) This realistic photo of the Gorre depot area was posed even before John started scenery on the layout. The delicate spoked wheels on the baggage wagons were made by inking dark lines on clear photographic film, then cutting out the circles.

(Left) The first G.D. was only 6'-8" long by 3'-7" wide. This first plan shows that John originally intended to place the turntable and enginehouse inside the loop. Later, he changed his mind and moved them outside the loop and to the front edge of the layout.

els were assembled from scratch or from individual commercial parts.

In a draft for an article that was never published, John wrote of the scarcity of materials and about making the best of it:

"Shortly before the end of World War II I came across the hobby of model railroading. At the time, of course, little in the way of supplies was available, so I started building with odds and ends, using raw materials such as cardboard, tin cans, and celluloid.

"Some people might think this was a disadvantage, but I believe it was a good thing. Instead of depending upon the manufacturers to do my thinking and modeling, I was encouraged to find out, by studying the prototype railroads, how things were made and what was correct.

"Take track walking as an example. I would wander by the railroad tracks and measure the sizes of things like the spacing between tracks, rail sizes used in different kinds of track, color of the roadbed, etc. On switches I'd see how the points were feathered and ground to fit against the stock rails. The result is that I measure my modeling against the prototype rather than against what is considered 'scale' in the hobby but actually far from it.

"When manufactured equipment did become available, I judged it by the accuracy of design and scale compared to the prototype. Ready-made track didn't look right to me. Ties were too perfectly spaced, too similar in size, and too large. Brass rail was brass in color, oversize, and with a head that was much too wide in relation to the height."

Reflecting upon his beginnings in the hobby, John wrote in a *Model Trains* article six years later: "When I first found out about this fascinating hobby of model railroading, late in

1944, I couldn't find a single model railroader around here. In old issues of the MODEL RAILROADER magazine I came across articles by Jim Dechert, who lived in Del Monte, a stone's throw from Monterey. But investigation found that Jim had moved back East, then to Santa Barbara, some 240 miles from here. This is unfortunate for my railroading interests as Jim is one of the real pioneers in HO. He was a driving force for the shift from third rail to two-rail distribution.

"This doesn't mean I'm still lost for companions in the hobby, for more recently a number of enthusiasts have joined the model railroad fraternity here. We are all newcomers and though we have lots of fun, we can always appreciate those with experience."

A model railroad club, the Monterey Peninsula Railroaders, was formed in 1946 with Allen Knight as President and Charles Rush as Secretary. The club planned to build a club layout in Knight's home, and John was appointed Construction Superintendent. During this period John was also occupied with building models at home in his small apartment and studio on Alvarado Street.

Building cars and structures. —— I call 1944 to 1946 the "tabletop" period in John's modeling. He had no layout, but he arranged the models he built on a low tabletop and photographed them against a sheet of card representing the sky. At first this background was plain blue, but in early 1948 John painted clouds upon it. It was used many times after that in John's published photos.

In this period of a year and a half John constructed about 14 freight and passenger cars, one locomotive (his famous Varney "Dockside" 0-4-0), nine structures, and numerous figures and detail accessories. All of the structures and about half of the cars were scratchbuilt, while the rest included various commercial parts.

All of these early models survived and found their way onto John's first and later layouts. In fact, if you study the photographs throughout this book, you can find most of them on the final Gorre & Daphetid, and John would enjoy watching you trace the individual models as they appeared on his various layouts.

In March 1946 John prepared photos for his first magazine article, which appeared in the July MODEL RAILROADER. In it, John told how to make model railroad photographs. He arranged some of his models on a plank of rough wallboard, then positioned a light to cast sharp shadows, simulating the sun. He added other, softer lighting to illuminate detail in the shadows, simulating skylight. In addition to photographing the scene with his large view camera, he made other photos of himself doing the work. He was a born teacher and his article warned of things not to do as well as giving advice on lighting and lens settings.

One magazine editor, upon seeing John's photos, assumed that John had a big layout. He was amazed to learn that John's only layout was a scene on a plank in a small apartment room!

Although model railroading in the United States began in New York and spread from the East Coast, a second, even faster-growing center of activity had developed in California in the late 1930s. John visited many home and club layouts and he made the acquaintance of most of the West Coast manufacturers, many of whom became his lifelong friends.

One of the friendships that developed was with George

Hook, who made Central Valley car trucks and other model products. George was a true gentleman, always helpful to anyone. Soon the little factory building John had built was dedicated to the Central Valley Model Works.

Another early friendship was with Gordon Varney, who made cars and locomotives in HO and, for a while, ¼" scale. John's acquaintance with Varney led to his making some remarkable advertising photos on both the old and new G.D. layouts in the 1950s but, in this earlier day, he made a few photos on the tabletop for Varney's catalog.

Planning the first G.D. —— If there was no space for even a modest layout in his small apartment, at least John could build a test track, and that is how the first Gorre & Daphetid began. He tried to make it as much of a complete railroad as he could, in spite of its very small size. Much detailed planning was done in 1945 before construction was begun.

One quality of John Allen that impresses me is that he prepared himself thoroughly for everything he did. Before starting his first layout, he read all the American and several overseas model railroad magazines to learn the techniques others had developed. He scrutinized other modelers' railroads and asked about their construction methods. In art school he had become familiar with materials that model railroaders might not think of using. His approach to modeling was to consider the techniques others used, try some of them and try variations of his own, then settle on the methods he considered most practical. While he could be patient when necessary, he preferred modeling methods that were fairly quick to implement and which would not require much maintenance later on.

Another unusual aspect of John's modeling personality was that he did not collect junk that he "might find a use for someday." If he acquired something, he knew exactly where it was going to be used. He felt keeping a scrap box of random materials was a waste of time and space.

His usual method of planning a new project was to think it over for some time while he did other things. Then he would make trial sketches on paper. If planning a layout, he would build a miniature of it using cardboard, balsa, and clay. If planning a structure, he would cut and fold a cardboard dummy of it and put it in place on the layout to see if the proportions were acceptable.

After a plan suited him, John went ahead with construction, rarely making changes in his design. He felt doing anything over again was a waste, because it should have been planned better at the start. "Changes are sometimes made in the unfinished portions," he wrote to the editor of *HO Model Trains*, "but the overall picture is known. I prefer to avoid making time-consuming changes to the work already done." He did as much construction as possible on his workbench, then carried the project to the layout.

John developed the track plan for the first Gorre & Daphetid around October 1945. He intended to build the layout in two stages: First he would construct a compact two-tier, two-lap oval with a small yard in front. After that he would add more framework at the one end so he could extend the yard, add a city, and build a return loop on a third tier. It would still be a small, portable layout.

After drawing the track diagram, John made two miniature models of the proposed layout. One model was of the framework and roadbed for the first stage. Every stick was

(Above left) **Except for the branch to Daphetid, John had completed laying track on the first G.D. by December 1946, shortly after moving into the house on Irving Street. The small station at Gorre in this photo shows up at Austin on the later G.D. layouts. (Above right) By early 1947 John had removed the ramp-like roadbed boards on the upper tier of the layout to make room for a graceful curved trestle over placid Taylor Lake. Note the temporary bridge at Gorre and the miniature layout model on the white card near the center of this photo.**

represented. The second miniature was larger because it included the yard extension and the top tier with return loop. Clay represented the terrain contours, and small blocks of wood represented the tall office buildings of a city within the loop. During construction John kept the track plan drawing and the two miniatures beside him as reference.

The track plan. —— The first G.D. was tiny, 3 feet 7 inches deep, and 6 feet 8 inches long. The small yard in front had three tracks that converged into the main line. The main line formed a two-lap, two-tier oval. From the yard it curved (in either direction) 180 degrees to a hidden ramp in back, then around another curve to cross over itself on a stone and timber viaduct above the yard. It returned to yard level again via a similar curve and ramp arrangement.

The sharpest curves had a radius of only 14 inches, but John said they could handle cars up to 54 scale feet long. The actual grades up or down the ramps were 2 percent, but to allow for the drag of the curves, John considered them "3 percent compensated." He superelevated (banked) the curves and added short easement spirals at each end.

A steeper branch, partly 3.5 percent, left the viaduct running counterclockwise, curving to the back of the layout. There the roadbed split to connect with the two ends of the proposed upper tier return loop.

Through his reading and study of other modelers' work, John realized that the open-grid method of framing offered more freedom in track location and scenery than a flat table-like top. Some years later John wrote notes for a book about scenery in which he warned new modelers against the flat top method of layout construction:

"Solid tabletop construction has many disadvantages and practically no advantages with the exception of the doubtful privilege of changing your mind at any stage of construction to extend track this way instead of that way."

He pointed out that solid-top construction used more material, was heavier, needed stronger framework, cost more, acted like a sounding board, and made access from below more difficult than an open grid. The solid top also restricted the modeler's ability to include up and down grades.

The framework was assembled from 1 x 2 lumber. Roadbed was band sawed from ¾" plywood. Individual white pine ties made by Bessey were glued in place. (Bessey was the first commercial supplier of stripwood for model railroaders.) John considered the track noisy, so never laid track directly on wood again. For later construction he placed a layer of Firtex insulation board on top of plywood, making two-layer roadbed.

Track laying was begun in the fall of 1946. Because John had limited space, he could work on the railroad in the photo studio but had to remove it completely when the studio was needed for photo work. Before long, John sold the studio and moved into a house on Irving Street. Since the house had its effect upon the G.D. railroad, I'll describe it next.

The long, narrow house. —— The trailer-like house was less than a mile northwest of downtown, near the canneries. It was about right for a young bachelor with modest spending habits. The house was a strange structure. Most of it was only 12 feet wide, but the house was 70 feet long, running down a narrow lot from the street to a back fence. There were fences on each side and, along the north flank, a narrow

Instead of locating the enginehouse and turntable inside the loop, John placed a simple industrial spur there. He built the first control panel into the framework, mounting it against the upper tier track along the front edge of the layout.

vegetable garden which John tended only a little more industriously than his garden at Shattuck Academy.

The floor area of the house was scarcely 1000 square feet, yet it was divided into eight tiny rooms arranged in an awkward end-to-end plan. To walk from the bedroom at the front to the bathroom at the rear John had to pass through the living room, another bedroom, a small dining room, the kitchen, a pantry, and yet another bedroom. The bathroom and living room were the largest rooms in the house, about 12 feet by 15 feet each.

At first, John planned to renovate the house, making an apartment for a renter in the rear and keeping the front part for himself. He would make the front bedroom into a den, the second bedroom into a new kitchen, and the dining room into

his own bedroom. Soon he abandoned that idea and kept the entire house for himself. He removed the wall between two of the middle rooms to make a 20-foot-long office, workshop, and studio. Later this became the railroad room.

John resumed construction of his portable railroad in the Irving Street house. By December 1946 enough track was in place to run a train around the main line. Rail was spiked to every sixth tie, but there was no skimping on the number of ties used. The first track switches were the type where the points, closure rails, and wing rails at the frog moved as a unit. The movable section pivoted midway between the points and the frog so that the wing rails closed against the frog on one side. In later construction, John used normal rigid-frog turnouts.

Automobile choke cables were popular for throwing turnouts at that time, so John connected the two most difficult to reach switches this way. He installed manually operated switch stands for other switches. Later on he powered the switches with electric, rotary-relay switch machines.

Since more space had become available, John planned to use it. He abandoned the plan for a return loop on the upper tier, and by February 1947 the junction and one leg of the roadbed for that loop were removed. This left a gap where a graceful curved trestle was to be built and freed a larger space for Taylor Lake. The upper tier would now become the main line to connect the original layout with the newly "discovered" territory.

John began adding scenic terrain cautiously, developing techniques as he went along. The method he adopted was to span the open spaces between tracks with ½"-wide strips of cardboard spaced about an inch apart. Each strip was bent up and down in several places to roughly parallel its neighbors. This way, the strips roughly described the desired terrain profile. The ends of the strips were attached to edges of the roadbed and to each other with waterproof glue or cellulose model airplane cement. Clothespins and thumbtacks held the strips until the glue dried.

To form the terrain surface, John dipped pieces of wrinkled magazine paper into a thin sizing and laid them over the cardboard ribs. For sizing John first used a starch solution, but later he preferred texture paint thinned with water to about the consistency of house paint. Texture paint is not really paint nor is it true plaster. Instead, it is a plaster-like

After reading about the methods other modelers had used, John developed his own scenery techniques for the first G.D. After erecting a light, simple framework of cardboard strips, he covered it with pieces of magazine paper that had been dipped in starch (left). After the starch dried, he brushed on a coat of texture paint (center). Before painting, he carved rock strata and fissures into the final thick texture-paint coat (right).

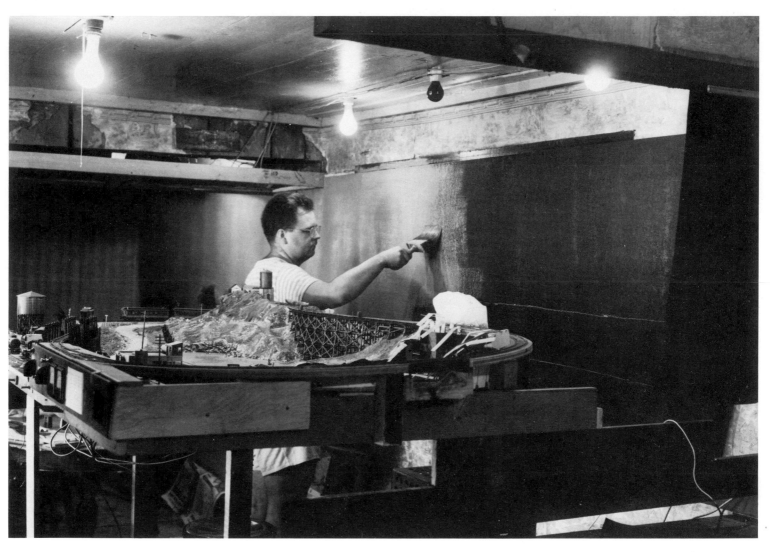

powder held together with a glue binder. Compared to plaster, texture paint dries slowly instead of setting while still wet, and it shrinks where plaster does not.

After the terrain hardened, John added two more coats of texture paint. He carved rock strata, masonry walls, and rivulets to simulate drainage courses in the last coat while it was still soft. Terrain coloring was done with light flat colors, either oils or watercolors. "Keep them light," he said. "Use lighter, bluer coloring on higher elevations and distant scenery.

"Add brush and trees. Put more plants in the wetter places. Vary the plant life so textures and colors are mixed. Use finer, smaller textures in the background." Foliage was held in place with Weldwood glue, then grass sawdust was sprinkled over the glue.

Before covering over the tunnels, John lined the inner walls with timber for about 50 scale feet from the portals. The trestle was made with piles of ⅛"-square stripwood mounted on wood blocks which represented concrete footings. A railing and water barrels added realism to the upper deck and the slight curve through the trestlework made the structure look longer than it really was.

The bottom of Taylor Lake was made in the same way as other terrain, but set into a hole in a frame of display card.

(Above) In 1947 John decided to make the G.D. permanent. He started by removing a section of kitchen wall (this photo was taken from the kitchen) and removing another wall (behind him here) entirely. Then he put up a long linoleum backdrop and painted it blue.

Just across Taylor Lake from the trestle was this tiny gristmill. The dam for the millpond was a convenient way for John to disguise the edge of the rippled glass "water," and he even animated the waterwheel with an inexpensive war-surplus electric motor.

(Above) This is one of several memorable photographs John took showing his old-time passenger train posed on the trestle over moonlit Taylor Lake. In this scene made about 1953 (after the G.D. was expanded), two night trains are about to meet at Daphetid siding.

(Opposite page, top) Number 8 had received her maroon paint and gold lettering by the time John posed this view in August of 1948. To gain extra space, he butted his tabletop display against the front edge of the layout and used his tabletop cloud background behind it.

(Far right) John revised his original Gorre & Daphetid track plan (page 40) to show the changes he had made during construction. In addition to moving the engine facilities outside the loop and replacing them with an industry, you'll see that the notation "D.G.& H. narrow gauge" now appears in two places in the Gorre yard.

(Right, adjacent) This July 1948 photo shows the layout before trees and bushes "grew" on the bare hills around Daphetid. John's 4-4-0, the Sergeant Ennis, had just been assembled and was still unpainted. Even unfinished modeling looked great when John was behind the camera!

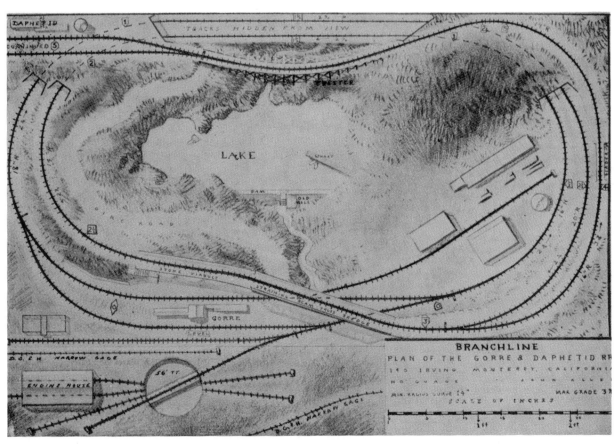

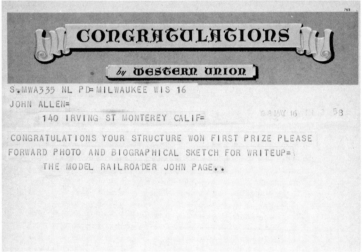

John's prizewinning G.D. enginehouse was a simple but extremely railroady structure that he built at a cost of less than a dollar (in 1948!). The photo, taken on the tabletop set, has a length of O gauge track and two O scale figures in the foreground to enhance the illusion of distance. The telegram was dated May 16, 1948.

After coloring the bottom, a plate of ripple glass was added to simulate water, and banks built upon it. Track reached Daphetid in July 1947, and shortly afterward John photographed his beautiful moonlight-on-the-lake scene.

Next, John attached linoleum to the back wall of the room and painted a sky backdrop upon it. The layout was pushed against that wall except when he needed access to the rear for construction.

A long, narrow strip of hardboard was attached to the front of the layout framework to hold control rheostats, a voltmeter, and an ammeter. Power was supplied by a large rectifier power supply, a rarity in those times as most modelers were still using storage batteries. Later, a control panel with a sloping front was installed.

Until 1947 the G.D. was supported on an old dining table with the middle leaves dropped out. Now John fitted it with its own 1 x 2 legs. It could still be pulled away from the wall. Working with the layout on the dining table had been backbreaking, and John was already beginning to complain about his back hurting. When he put legs under the layout, he raised it considerably higher to about 50 inches above the floor. In addition to being more comfortable to work on, there were other advantages, as John wrote:

"I believe most of the small pike modelers are ignoring one of the principal advantages of the small layout. This is placing it at a high, eye-level elevation. On a large layout you must place the track at a lower elevation so operators can see all of the route. But on the small pike you have no far distant objects...If you place the layout high, it will look like it goes on and on."

The terrain was completed about December 1947. It had taken nearly two years to complete the original G.D., largely because John was also spending time on house improvements and building rolling stock. It was also because John had a lifetime ahead of him and there was no need to hurry. Instead, he took his time and had fun building carefully.

The concept develops. ——— The G.D. track plan was modified slightly in early 1948: "Originally the turntable and enginehouse were planned inside the oval near the lake," John wrote in a caption for *HO Monthly* magazine, "but when the G.D. gained more area, they were placed in front of Gorre station." By the time John added the enginehouse, he was planning even more extensive enlargements.

Although a concept for the G.D. was a part of its earliest planning, the concept grew and shifted as John constructed track, structures, locomotives, and miniature figures. The railroad's character really began to form itself during 1947. Gradually, the G.D. came to be an un-modernized railroad in a modern period. John explained in a letter to Elliot Kahn:

"As you pointed out, my own railroad has many, many

This night scene reveals much of the interior detail of the Gorre enginehouse. Of it, John wrote: "The enginehouse crew is working overtime getting the Charles Rush, Number 1 [lower right], ready for the railroad's 25th Anniversary celebration. The railroad uses 12-to-1 fast time, so time passes quickly."

To enhance the illusion of depth, John once again posed one of his O scale figures in the foreground of this scene on the Gorre viaduct. The tracks in the foreground and the backdrop painting are part of the second, expanded G.D. (Chapter 4), but all other modeling shown here was part of John's original 3′-7″ by 6′-8″ layout.

inaccuracies. My railroad modeling is after all just a hobby and for fun and no attempt is made to model museum pieces. My railroads do not follow specific prototypes.

"They are freelance railroads in a mythical Western section of the U.S. Since the lines are small, old-fashioned railroads, it is supposed that much of our equipment is purchased secondhand from other more modern railroads. There is no attempt to make a period setting, but naturally on such a line equipment and buildings are old, run-down, and obsolete though more modern equipment could find its way onto the line."

The reason John spoke of his "railroads" in plural was that he was planning some narrow gauge, the Devil's Gulch & Helengon Railroad. We'll come to that in a moment.

More locomotives, and a prizewinning enginehouse. ———

In June 1947 the G.D. acquired its second locomotive, a Mantua 4-4-0 called the "Belle of the Eighties." In those days it cost less than $15 for the kit, which took about 6 hours to assemble and break in. John gave it the number 8 and named it the *Sergeant Ennis*.

Next John assembled a Strombecker wood locomotive kit. This model was a very early 2-2-0 design, vintage 1835. The model was sold as a toy, all wood and non-powered. This engine was to represent the G.D.'s "most ancient" locomotive. John found some metal wheels for it for electrical pickup so he could add a working headlight. (From the beginning, all G.D. rolling stock was lighted when appropriate.) The engine, Number 1, was named the *Charles Rush*, honoring the

  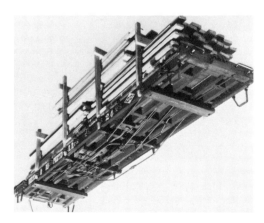

(Left) Cliff Grandt completed this beautiful scratchbuilt O scale Heisler locomotive after John had photographed it to show several areas where it could be improved. (Middle and right) John also built these On3 freight cars for Cliff. The photos were taken in February 1949.

first secretary of the new model railroad club in Monterey.

Engines need an enginehouse where they can be stored and serviced. Building one became the next major project on the G.D.

"So realistic is this enginehouse that it has the birds fooled." That was the beginning of the caption under the photo of John Allen's new two-stall rectangular enginehouse in the July 1948 MODEL RAILROADER. The structure won first prize for structures in the magazine's annual model contest. (The contest later became a feature of the National Model Railroad Association's annual convention.)

The G.D. enginehouse was not the first structure ever to be "weathered" with nail stains, smoke smudges, miniature pigeons and pigeon droppings, and broken windows, but it was the first such model to win an American model railroad contest. It influenced many modelers, for they discovered that a weathered model appears more realistic and detailed than the same model would appear in immaculate condition.

John began building the enginehouse in November 1947, and he described its construction in three articles in *Model Craftsman* (now *Railroad Model Craftsman*) beginning in October 1948. The design was influenced by but not copied from some of the O scale designs of modeler R.G. Kann who operated the Model Structures firm in nearby Santa Cruz. For his HO model John wanted large windows, including a few skylights so viewers could look into the building from above. The enginehouse was lighted and furnished with workbenches and tools.

The wall material was simply bristol board. John figured the cost of all materials was about 98 cents. After scribing siding boards with an ice pick, John rubbed paint on with a cloth, intentionally letting it streak. Next the door and window openings were cut and stripwood trim added. To simulate a foundation, John set small stones into glue along the base of each wall.

The aging was done with powdered chalk scraped from artist's pastel crayons. John used light, earthy colors, brushing the powder on. Where more coloring was wanted, John rubbed the powder with a finger, then brushed on more.

Windows were glazed with old photo film. The emulsion was removed with sodium carbonate, and when dry, window mullions were drawn onto the film with colored poster paint. Shingles were made of construction paper. The paper was streaked irregularly with paint, and then an edge was nicked to almost separate individual shingles. The edge was then cut away as a strip and applied to the roof, making a row of shingles that looked like they were individual. Roof gutters were stripwood channel, downspouts were solid metal, and pin heads simulated doorknobs.

As he wound up his construction story, John realized he was becoming a teacher. "One or two models of this caliber should change the entire atmosphere of your model pike. It will give you the incentive to get your layout in good running order," he wrote.

The enginehouse propelled John Allen into the model railroad limelight. From then on more visitors came to Monterey and more readers asked magazine editors for John Allen features. I had taken photos of some of the prizewinning models that year, and I went to Monterey to visit John the following year. From then on we were friends.

Cliff Grandt and his Heisler.

—— While construction continued on the enlarged G.D., John made occasional trips to visit other modelers and model railroad clubs. In Emeryville, near Oakland, he photographed the largest model railroad of its time, the O scale layout built by the East Bay Model Engineers Society. A large HO layout was also under construction. John met a number of the members and particularly enjoyed discussing the hobby with Cliff Grandt. Cliff was a mechanical genius, John an artistic genius, and each became an influence on the other. Later on, Cliff developed the "Grandt Line" of model parts and mechanisms.

John and Cliff frequently exchanged the products of their workmanship, Cliff making a few metal parts for John and John building and painting wood models for Cliff. The G.D.'s Strombecker 2-2-0 locomotive was crude compared to his other G.D. models, so in 1948 John decided to build a better "oldest G.D. loco." This was a 4-2-0 entirely scratchbuilt except for wheels and lamp bulb. Cliff helped by making a mechanism that fitted into a high-side gondola car to push the motorless engine. John made the rest. The new number 2 was a much better model than the old number 1.

Cliff Grandt tells how John used a camera to help Cliff improve his modelwork. Cliff built an O scale model of a Heisler geared locomotive. John photographed the model, then made a clear 8" x 10" enlargement from the negative. "Take this," said John, "and look it over with a magnifying glass. Whenever you can tell from the photo that the locomotive is a model rather than the prototype, you may be able to improve upon the modelwork."

Cliff says he was amazed at how many little things were giveaways. A tiny screw head he thought was well hidden showed noticeably. A compressor that had been carefully made with 12 parts looked crude. Cliff rebuilt the model, this time hiding the screw, and making a new compressor with 69 parts as well as many other changes. The rebuilt model won first prize in the annual MODEL RAILROADER contest in 1949.

John won an honorable mention in that same contest with a narrow gauge cattle car he had built. Devil's Gulch & Helengon car number 56 had a built-in sag simulating an old car with loose truss rods. It was homebuilt except for couplers, ladders, and the trucks which were re-gauged TT trucks. The lower portion of the car was realistically stained with white disinfectant.

In 1949 John built two O scale narrow gauge freight cars for Cliff Grandt. They were accurate models for which Cliff made some of the metal parts. John wrote to MODEL RAILROADER: "This was my first attempt in a larger than 3.5 mm [HO] scale."

For two years or so beginning in 1947, John was active in narrow gauge modeling, which brings us to Chapter 4.

Narrow gauge

"I'm not a strict prototype modeler. To me, half the fun is cogitating and planning. I'd just as soon take a feature I like from one car and put it on another as long as the practice is logical. I'm far more interested in general character than specific details. This may be one of the reasons narrow gauge fascinates me. It has few prototype standards. Each shop foreman used the tools on hand and his own ideas; so the equipment developed character."

A STRONG INTEREST in narrow gauge modeling figured prominently in John Allen's model railroad activity from 1947 well into the decade of the 1950s. The standard gauge (56½" between the rails) Gorre & Daphetid was joined by John's HOn3 (36" between the rails) Devil's Gulch & Helengon Railroad.

Beginning in 1947. John built several narrow gauge cars. The cars were scratchbuilt except for trucks because no HOn3 kits or parts were yet available. He traded two or three of these cars with other modelers. including Larry and Gladys Grabert of Long Beach. They were good friends of John's and were active in promoting narrow gauge modeling in HOn3. Larry conducted a narrow gauge column in *HO Monthly* in which John was mentioned occasionally.

For cars John soon needed track, which came next.

The Devil's Gulch & Helengon. —— During 1948 John knew he would eventually expand the G.D. layout into half of the large studio room in the Irving Street house. but plans for how he would arrange it were still going around in his head. To avoid putting HOn3 track where it might interfere with the future needs of the standard gauge. he started building the narrow gauge across the aisle from the original layout in the north corner of the room.

This is a color version of one of John Allen's famous black-and-white advertising photos for Varney Scale Models. In it, Gorre & Daphetid switcher number 12, a kit-built Roundhouse-brand 0-6-0, is about to meet a long drag freight headed by John's parts-built 4-10-0, number 34. The scene is the entrance to the three-track tunnel on the expanded G.D.

and an expanding G.D.

After building three narrow gauge boxcars, John added a third rail to one of the tracks at Gorre, butted a board with a length of HOn3 track up against the layout, and took this photo in January 1948.

The Devil's Gulch & Helengon first saw the light of day in July 1948 on a 1 foot by 6 foot shelf above John's workbench. The aisle (actually, it was the doorway to the kitchen) between the shelf and the G.D. was considered Devil's Gulch. Later on it was to be spanned by a removable bridge.

Helengon, on the new shelf, was a short, four-track yard in the shadow of towering Mount Alexander. John described Helengon in the December 1949 MODEL RAILROADER as a "Shoot 'em up and hang 'em tough western mining and lum-ber camp town." Mount Alexander was not much more than a bas-relief stuck to the wall; 8 inches deep and 30 inches wide, it rose 21 inches above the tracks.

As you can see in John's sketch (and in the track plan of the expanded Gorre & Daphetid, pages 62 and 63), Helengon yard had two tracks that led onto the turntable, thus eliminating the need for one track switch. An enginehouse track also led away from the turntable, and a long spur track bent around the corner to reach a lumber mill.

On the main layout benchwork the narrow gauge from Helengon was to skirt behind the original layout and run through a wye to reach Gorre from the left, snaking its terminal tracks between some of the standard gauge tracks. No three-rail track was planned, but in Gorre the narrow gauge was to have an unloading track directly above a standard gauge track for gravity transfer of minerals. A meandering switchback from near Devil's Gulch led upgrade over a timber bridge to the site of a mine on the flank of Mousebelly Mountain.

Two narrow gauge yard tracks were laid in Gorre late in 1950 after the standard gauge railroad had begun expanding into more of the room space, but a through narrow gauge connection from Helengon was not completed until July 1952, a matter of months before the Irving Street layout was torn up.

The HOn3 branch to the wharves at Grabert was never built. John sketched the route and explained how a D.G.& H. train might operate over the Helengon-to-Gorre route in his narrow gauge round robin letter of November 1949:

"There will be no loops in the track plan or any apparently unnecessary curves (not justified by terrain). The wye turns trains or engines around for two of the stations and there is a turntable at the third.

"A loco pulls out of the enginehouse or siding at Helengon, then pulls out the cars for the day's train to Gorre and the river piers. After makeup is nearly done, it picks up the empty ore cars and pushes them up to the mine. Then it picks up the loaded ore cars and puts them into the train. It backs with the combination caboose-baggage-passenger car to the station to load passengers and baggage. Then it starts down the line for Gorre. It pulls into the branch of the wye as

To build Helengon, John erected a chest-high shelf above his workbench in the north corner of the railroad room.

John first made a miniature model of Helengon yard, shown here, then set about building the intricate three-way stub switch.

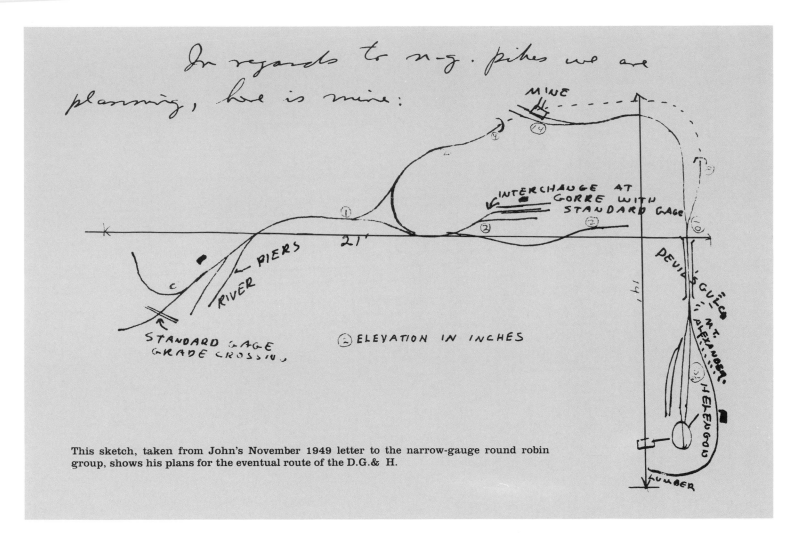

In regards to n-g. pikes we are planning, here is mine:

MINE

INTERCHANGE AT GORRE WITH STANDARD GAGE

DEVIL'S GULCH

MT. ALEXANDER

HELENGON

RIVER PIERS

21'

C

STANDARD GAGE GRADE CROSSING

(z) ELEVATION IN INCHES

LUMBER

This sketch, taken from John's November 1949 letter to the narrow-gauge round robin group, shows his plans for the eventual route of the D.G.& H.

though heading for the wharves, but backs into Gorre instead.

"After switching for the return trip at Gorre, it backs to the wharves to drop off and pick up cars there. Then it heads for Helengon, unless emergency loads from the wharf have to be taken to Gorre. At Helengon it switches cars to their proper sidings, then to the turntable and engine track for the night.

"I figure it will take close to 12 hours scale time (one real hour) to make the day's trip. Grades will be up to 4 percent, curves 12″ radius on the main and 10″ on some sidings. Trains will be 6 to 8 cars long. I have not yet decided what kind of automatic couplers the narrow gauge line will use."

Humor arrives on the narrow gauge. ——— John's modeling personality was genial but largely humorless until he became interested in narrow gauge. Except for the old time locomotives, his original standard gauge models were reminiscent of a rural branch line of the 1920s. By contrast, anything might be found on the narrow gauge—no matter how strange. For the D.G.& H. John built swaybacked cars, fat conductors, engines with antlers on the headlight, a diesel salesman lynched from a bridge, and curious creatures such as Emma the stegosaurus and a giant O scale man who worked at Gorre. Both could switch cars of any gauge.

This photo, taken as part of the G.D.'s 50th anniversary festivities, shows the spectacular painting of Devil's Gulch that John rendered on the kitchen door panel between the main layout and Mount Alexander. The "Chief Cuss and General Manager," as John called himself, posed at the controls.

(Left) The route and physical layout of the Devil's Gulch & Helengon were reproduced on John's D.G.& H. passes. (Below and right) This two-page spread from the April 1950 issue of MODEL RAILROADER magazine recounts the zany antics of some of John's "little people" on his narrow gauge D.G.& H. and on his friend Larry Grabert's Thief River & Chug Water Ry., another HOn3 railroad.

Narrow Gauge, Broad Beams

An exchange of letters between two West Coast narrow gauge tycoons about a weighty problem

THIEF RIVER & CHUG WATER RY.
LONG BEACH, CALIF.

Mar. 1, 1950

Mr. John Allen, General Manager
Gorre & Daphetid RR.
Monterey, Calif.

Dear John:

This letter will serve to introduce Horace P. Vestibule III. Mr. Vestibule desires employment as a conductor on the G&D.

Horace has been in passenger service on our line for 2 weeks 1 day 3 hours. He has been an honest, conscientious, trustworthy employee. I heartily recommend him to you; indeed my feelings toward Horace can hardly be expressed in words. No one will be more pleased than I if you'll hire him, except possibly the citizens of Burp Hollow, home of the Smaltz Brewery. It seems that Horace can consume our local brew faster than the brewery working three shifts can turn it out. This has left many people hereabouts feeling very unhappy, and very dry. Yesterday a committee of irate gentlemen called on me and hinted that it would be a patriotic duty for the TR&CW to persuade Horace to leave these parts. Or else — .

If you don't have a run for Horace, perhaps you can tap him and open a beer joint.

Yours,

LARRY GRABERT
General Manager

GORRE & DAPHETID RR.
MONTEREY, CALIF.

Mar. 8, 1950

Mr. Larry Grabert, General Manager
Thief River & Chug Water Ry.
Long Beach 6, Calif.

Dear Larry:

Thanks for sending us Horace P. V. No. 3. In return we are sending you our G&D narrow gauge car No. 311 for repairs.

After using a tape measure around Horace, we decided against making him a conductor. Our car aisles are only 2 ft. wide. A broth of a lad like Horace needs more elbow room. We can't afford to be sued by passengers

John Allen

who have been squeezed out through windows and pushed out of car ends as our conductor surges down the aisle. So we hired Horace as a yardmaster.

You were right in saying that he's conscientious. He made regular and thorough inspections. We couldn't understand why we suddenly had so many swaybacked narrow gauge cars, until yesterday a brakeman spotted Horace inspecting one. As proof, I enclose a photograph (see opposite page) of Horace in action on a car. One glance at it should stifle your impulse to send us a bill for repairs. Why didn't you warn us in the first place?

Sincerely,

JOHN ALLEN

John Allen

THIEF RIVER & CHUG WATER RY.
LONG BEACH, CALIF.

Mar. 10, 1950

Dear John:

We're truly sorry that H. P. has turned out to be a train-wrecker. We've put No. 311 in the shops.

In case future repairs are needed after one of Horace's ramblings, we are sending you a crackerjack repairman, Archibald Peter Van Slurp. "Arch-Bar Pete," as he is known, has worked in our shops 30 years. Incidentally, he and Horace are old buddies, and Arch-Bar Pete is probably the only man in California whose capacity matches Horace's. I'm sure you'll find them a simply devastating team.

Yours,

LARRY GRABERT

GORRE & DAPHETID RR.
MONTEREY, CALIF.

Mar. 16, 1950

Dear Larry:

"Devastating" ain't the word! These lads are atomic — in effect, if not size. Where do you find these types — in the ocean?

Arch-Bar was so happy to see his old tosspot buddy he insisted on being hired as Horace's assistant, promising to do repair work on his own time. Rather dubiously, we agreed.

Almost immediately we noticed a deterioration of our narrow gauge rolling stock. Cars developed inexplicable sways, warps, and rattles. We put railroad dicks on the trail. Our dicks discovered that Horace and Arch-Bar Pete, those mastodonic bosom pals, liked to chew the fat, so they inspected cars together. Horace, being of superior rank, chose the car

floors, while Arch-Bar inspected roofs. To strengthen themselves during their labors, they took along a little refreshment and dragooned George to wheel it along.

I'm enclosing a photo (see above) taken by one of our detectives, and tomorrow we'll be sending you eight more cars for repairs.

If you have any more trusted, loyal, efficient, etc., etc., employees whose services you can dispense with, kindly refrain from sending them to us.

Sincerely,

JOHN ALLEN

GORRE & DAPHETID RR.
MONTEREY, CALIF.

Mar. 24, 1950

Dear Larry:

We here at G&D have always prided ourselves in understanding our employees' personal viewpoints; we have found that treating their individual problems as our own pays. In line with this policy the board of directors, at a special meeting yesterday, voted the use of two specially equipped, heavy-duty cars capable of transporting our new yardmaster and his assistant over the line without mishap or too much damage to company property.

As a result, G&D has two more loyal, satisfied employees. The boys are especially happy because their new equipment enables them to carry along enough fuel and refreshment for a full day's inspection trip.

Our personnel department is sending you the enclosed photo (see below) of Horace and Arch-Bar with their new equipment, fueled and ready to start a hard day's labor. Now everything is fine.

Sincerely,

JOHN ALLEN

John Allen

John fantasized how the coming of the narrow gauge would affect the standard gauge railroad in a piece he wrote for *HO Model Trains* magazine for February 1950:

"And there's the impending Devil's Gulch & Helengon narrow gauge ready to push shortly into Gorre. Will it be a stiff and dangerous competitor or a helpful feeder line? Can the G.D. get control of its stock? Or merge? Both railroads are pushing their tracks forward vigorously in a race to secure more advantageous rights of way. Competition is keen and construction gangs are armed. The G.D. has the advantage of reaching Gorre first but the D.G.& H. boys are mountain people, long accustomed to dropping squirrels with shots squarely between the eyes. There is no ICC to settle disputes.

"What will the future be when the gasoline wagons start fighting for the transportation business?

"Several of my cars run on other model railroad lines and theirs on mine. What happens when a wreck ensues and one of the cars is damaged? Do I meekly repair it? Or do I threaten the owning railroad for damages? The G.D. threatens suit, especially if it has the weaker side of the case."

As John's humorous escapades increased, so did his knowledge of model railroad technique. After he wrote numerous provocative letters to the editors of the model railroad magazines, one editor challenged him to make a contribution if he wished to criticize. John replied that, "I like to criticize but I don't like to write." He became a frequent contributor anyway.

John told how he built Mount Alexander in the December 1949 MODEL RAILROADER. "Natural objects such as mountains have no repetitious geometric lines and angles to complicate the perspective as do man-made objects. This makes it possible to create the illusion [of a large mountain in a small space] by resorting to size and color perspective rather than linear perspective.

"Trees can be all sizes but it is normal to think of trees in the distance as being the same height as those nearby. Reducing their size as they are placed higher on the modeled mountain creates the illusion of distance. Houses or people placed in the scene also have to be reduced proportionately.

"As I worked up the mountain, I weakened the intensity of the color, gradually arriving at pale blues and violets. This was done under the same light that would later be used to illuminate the finished scene." John explained: "Colors take on different values under different types of light. Therefore, the lighting was installed first."

The narrow gauge round robin. —— In the late 1940s little narrow gauge modeling had been done in HO scale, and those in HOn3 were a hardy band of pioneers. In December 1948 John initiated a round robin letter series among eight or nine modelers who were then active in HOn3.

John started round robin letters more than once. He would write something he felt should provoke interest among the others, the next fellow would add his comments, and then the next. The letter would go around and around until the various members either dropped out or had no more to say on its subject. John acted as a sort of whip, trying to keep up the enthusiasm of the others, yet at the same time he complained how much work it was answering letters.

John's first round robin series was with this narrow gauge group. Not all the letters have survived, but the series

One of John's best-remembered whimsies was Emma, the work stegosaurus. John wrote that she was "not very smart, but obliging and strong." One advantage of Emma was that she could switch both standard and narrow gauge cars.

seems to have started in December 1948 first among narrow gauge standards committee members and then among others interested in any aspect of narrow gauge. By August 1950 the narrow gauge letters faded out. Later, John started at least two other round robin series with modelers interested in operation.

John's willingness to help others entangled him in an awkward situation related to the round robin letters. In 1948 John and Larry Grabert decided they should adopt a common HOn3 wheel standard between them so that "we could run our equipment on each other's railroads." Naturally they wrote about it to the others and that started a chain of events.

John said afterward: "Since then one thing led to another, and now neither of us have time to build the railroad, but you should see our correspondence files. We both regret we didn't keep our mouths shut. Neither of us cared whether

Mount Alexander, near Helengon, was the major landmark on the Devil's Gulch & Helengon narrow gauge. The scenery included a rickety hanging footbridge, and the mountain extended right into the full-height door painting of Devil's Gulch.

"Never let it be said that there is reason for animosity between rail-roaders of different scales," John wrote. As if to prove his point, he obligingly built an O scale man and put him to work switching cars in the yard at Gorre, with a couple of HO figures looking on!

When a diesel salesman came to call, the unsympathetic G.D. crew summarily lynched him from Hangman's Bridge, near Daphetid. The two figures with sombreros are the notorious Sowfoot brothers, "two of the fattest men in the area," John wrote.

Not until 1952 could D.G.& H. narrow gauge trains roll around this sweeping curve and into the terminal at Gorre. The rocks in the center and right of this photo were props that John often used to disguise unfinished openings in the scenery.

A rather eccentric teakettle to say the least, D.G.& H. number 3 sported a fabric awning in lieu of a cab, antlers on the headlight, and a six-gun-toting engineer with a big handlebar moustache. For years the 3-spot was the only power on the narrow gauge.

Gorre & Daphetid President M.H. Vanderlip rode in cool shade and style beneath the convertible top of his private rail auto and inspection car. Powered by a brushless "gap-ring" motor built by Cliff Grandt, the G.D.'s smallest piece of equipment hummed merrily along once John gave it a push to get it started. John wrote that its fictional "prototype" probably needed an occasional push, too.

HOn3 became popular or not, but we found ourselves finally holding the bear by the tail and no way to let it go."

Because of his enthusiasm and contact with other narrow gauge modelers, John was appointed chairman of a subcommittee to study HOn3 wheel and track standards by NMRA narrow gauge chairman Jack Alexander. This was in 1949. The existing HO gauge standards were too coarse if HOn3 was to satisfy careful modelers.

This kite-flying HO figure was the subject of one of John's earliest articles. The secret was the kite string: John used stainless-steel fishing leader so that the "string," not the wind, held the kite aloft.

John felt that finer standards were needed if the models were to look right. He also felt that such finer standards would have to be set soon, before manufacturers spent money on tooling using the existing standards. By January 1950 all but one of his six-man committee agreed upon new recommendations, so that should have been that.

The one committee member who did not concur set out to undermine the work of the others by writing letters to manufacturers, magazine editors, and other NMRA members arguing that the manufacturers would be upset by any change in standards and would stop making any HOn3 supplies at all. (This was tilting at windmills, for at the time, the only manufacturer supplying HOn3 wheels was M. Dale Newton—who was quite willing to make a change.)

John and the other committee members wrote tactful letters that prevented the smouldering conflict from igniting. The dissenting member resigned, and eventually time healed the wounds. The committee had wheels made to its proposed standards and tested them until the members could agree on new specifications. After further delay, HOn3 standards were adopted, this to the benefit of HO narrow gauge modeling ever since.

Narrow gauge or standard? —— In the early 1950s John realized that it was not likely for a model railroader to keep up narrow gauge and standard gauge systems equally well. One or the other will get most of the attention, and the unfavored one may even be neglected. John did not want that, so he decided to keep his narrow gauge—and later his trolley system—simple both in layout and motive power roster. The standard gauge Gorre & Daphetid got most of his attention and most of the real estate in G.D. territory.

He did build more rolling stock after 1948, including D.G.& H. engine 3, a fine free-lance model based on a Porter

John designed this stamp to commemorate the G.D., and placed small photocopies of it alongside the regular postage on about 20 letters sent to fellow modelers. Upon learning the practice was illegal, John issued no more stamps.

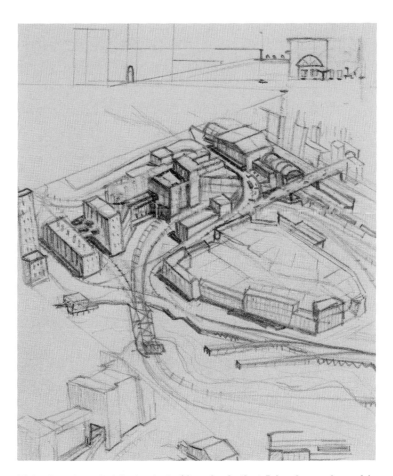

This planning sketch, typical of hundreds that John drew, shows his concept for the city area on the expanded Gorre & Daphetid. A mirror was to double the apparent size of the terminal at Great Divide, just as such a mirror was later used on John's final layout.

design. It was mounted on a Lindsay mechanism in 1949. The following year he started an even finer engine, D.G.& H. number 1, using parts made for him by Cliff Grandt. Before it was completed this locomotive was stolen by a visitor during an open house. You can see it in the photo John took in 1952 showing all the motive power of the G.D. and D.G.& H., page 126.

By 1950 the D.G.& H. had built eight freight cars; a combination passenger, baggage, and mail car; and a caboose. Both the standard and narrow gauge rosters included rail autos. The G.D. had its "President's car" and the D.G.& H. featured an elongated charabanc-style bus. Dubbed the "Ruptured Duck," the D.G.& H. car resembled the narrow gauge "Galloping Geese" of the Rio Grande Southern.

The D.G.& H. main line at the Irving Street house was completed in 1952, but the branch to the harbor at Grabert was never built. After John moved to Cielo Vista Terrace some HOn3 track was laid at Gorre on the new layout. A third rail was laid in the otherwise standard gauge second tier track from above Sowbelly to Helengon Gap, but the loop there and other essential HOn3 track was never completed.

In 1963 the narrow gauge round robin was revived briefly and John summarized his narrow gauge modeling:

"It's been three years since this letter last went through and I thought it long dead. Glad to see it got a new lease on life and some new members, welcome.

"Since the last letter I've done nothing in narrow gauge, in fact very little since I moved some 10 years ago and tore out the old D.G.& H. About all I have done since starting this layout has been to put in the dual gauge (so as not to hold back the standard gauge) and build one or two freight cars. I have digressed to a one loco stud, again, since a visitor lifted one about a year ago. I still plan to finish the narrow gauge, someday, in fact all the ties are in and most track, but then they have been that way for years. So I don't want to sail under false colors as a working modeler of narrow gauge; perhaps it woud be best if I dropped off and allowed room for a more aggressive worker?

"Everyone who develops two gauges or scales works toward developing one to a greater extent and subordinating the other. Space and the scarcity of operators as well as maintenance governs, so I have favored the standard gauge system. Both have equal interest to me. Other than the D.& R.G., narrow gauge is light railroading, and I see little difference between it and old, old time standard gauge. The problems are the same and the equipment can be similar."

The G.D. expands. —— During the next few paragraphs, let us assume it is early fall 1948. John needs more space so the narrow gauge line can reach Gorre to transfer loads to the standard gauge; he needs more real estate for the structures he has and is still building; and he needs more track to

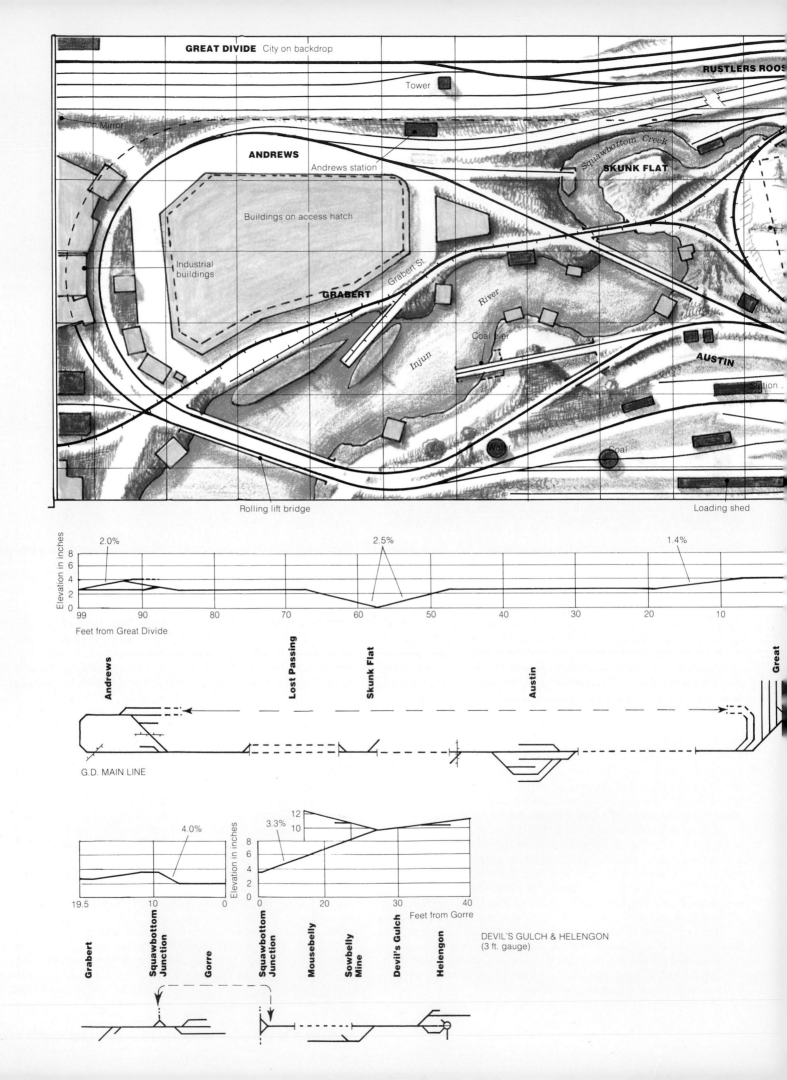

GREAT DIVIDE City on backdrop

RUSTLERS ROOS

Tower

Mirror

ANDREWS

Andrews station

Squawbottom Creek

SKUNK FLAT

Buildings on access hatch

Industrial buildings

Grabert St.

GRABERT

River

Coal pier

Injun

AUSTIN

Station

Water

Coal

Rolling lift bridge

Loading shed

2.0%   2.5%   1.4%

Elevation in inches

99   90   80   70   60   50   40   30   20   10

Feet from Great Divide

Andrews   Lost Passing   Skunk Flat   Austin   Great

G.D. MAIN LINE

4.0%   3.3%

12
10
Elevation in inches
8
6
4
2

19.5   10   0   0   20   30   40

Feet from Gorre

DEVIL'S GULCH & HELENGON
(3 ft. gauge)

Grabert   Squawbottom Junction   Gorre   Squawbottom Junction   Mousebelly   Sowbelly Mine   Devil's Gulch   Helengon

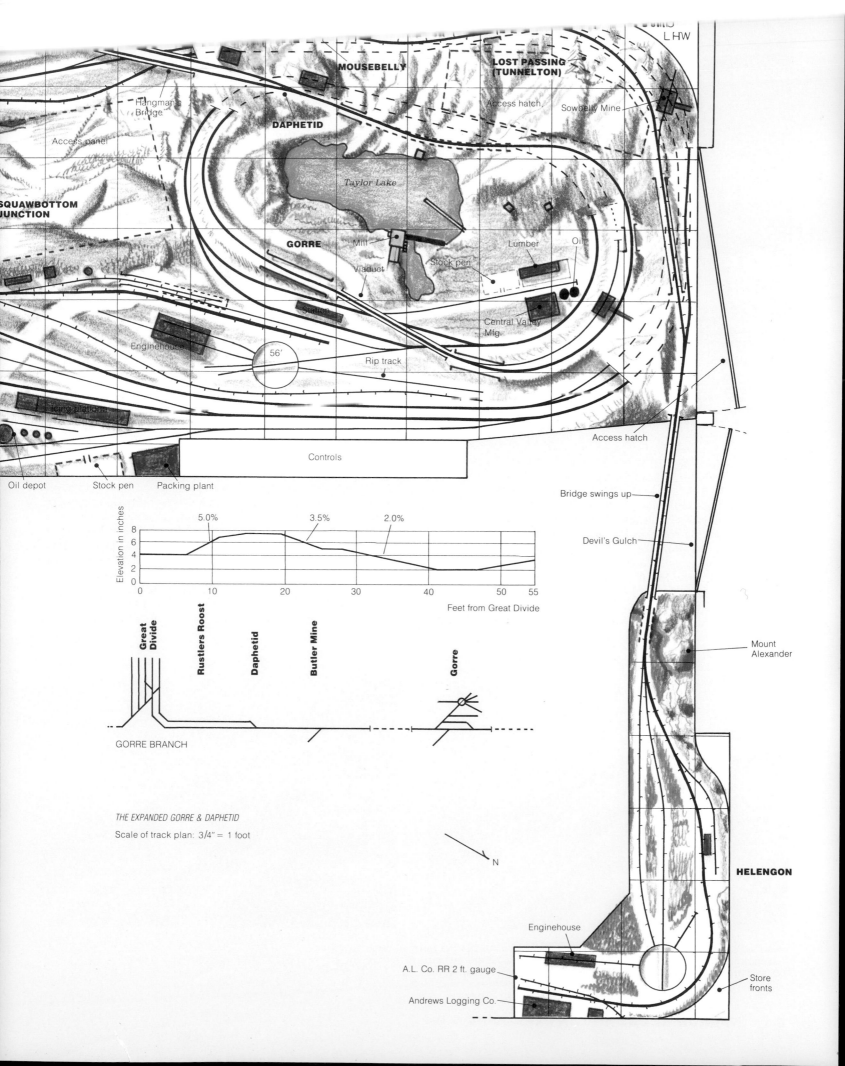

MOUSEBELLY

LOST PASSING
(TUNNELTON)

L HW

DAPHETID

Access hatch

Sowbelly Mine

Hangman's
Bridge

Access panel

Taylor Lake

SQUAWBOTTOM
JUNCTION

GORRE

Mill

Lumber

Oil

Viaduct

Stock pen

Central Valley
Mfg.

Station

56'

Enginehouse

Rip track

Access hatch

Icing platform

Controls

Bridge swings up

Oil depot   Stock pen   Packing plant

Devil's Gulch

	5.0%	3.5%	2.0%		

Elevation in inches

8
6
4
2
0

0   10   20   30   40   50   55

Feet from Great Divide

Mount
Alexander

Great
Divide

Rustlers Roost

Daphetid

Butler Mine

Gorre

GORRE BRANCH

HELENGON

THE EXPANDED GORRE & DAPHETID

Scale of track plan: 3/4" = 1 foot

N

Enginehouse

A.L. Co. RR 2 ft. gauge

Andrews Logging Co.

Store
fronts

(Above) John began expanding the G.D. late in 1948. Here, in July 1949, the original layout has been positioned on the new benchwork, and the extended main line connected to it. (Right) This view, looking southeast through the access panel from the kitchen, shows the classification yard at Great Divide, the mirror along the far edge of the layout, and the earliest beginnings of John's exquisite painted backdrop.

rationalize the expanding rolling stock roster. During the time John was busy building the Helengon terminal for the D.G.& H., he was also exploring routes for it to reach the G.D. and for the G.D. itself to be extended.

His plan has crystalized, and the railroad will occupy half of the double room in the middle of the house. The new layout will be 20 feet 6 inches long by 6 feet 6 inches deep.

The new plan includes the old layout, almost intact. John wrote about this to *HO Model Trains*: "The well constructed small railroad does not need to be discarded when a larger area becomes available. It is usually practical to incorporate it right into the larger pike as a branch line and operation can

continue while the new right of way is under construction."

John realized that it was not best to have tracks paralleling the aisleways or room walls any more than necessary, so he twisted the original layout a little clockwise in relation to the background wall. He arranged the new main lines to surround the old layout; in back they would be hidden under terrain supporting a mine on a narrow gauge spur, in front of Gorre they would look like part of the yard, but make no connection.

You might expect the original "branch line" to connect to the new main line here at Gorre. Not so. Instead, Gorre becomes the terminal of the branch. From here trains must

Even without scenery, the mirror along the southeast wall of the railroad room vastly expanded the G.D. To show how much, John covered the mirror with paper for one photo (above left), then removed the paper for the comparison (above right).

One block would lift away from an access hatch in the benchwork, while another group would be against a large mirror at the left end of the room. The mirror was to double the apparent size of the city and the whole railroad empire.

My first visit. —— My first visit to the G.D. was in August 1949, after the new area of the layout had been under construction for about eight months. I had driven south from San Francisco and it was already dark outside. John knew I was coming, of course. He had his overalls on because he had been coloring terrain. He was chubby, 6 feet tall, and a very congenial host. We chatted in his neat living room, then went into the railroad room for a long evening of exchanging views and experiences.

I learned that the expansion which was now in progress had begun around December 1948. Obviously it had proceeded fairly quickly. A little more than half of the eventual framework was already in place. The mirror at Great Divide was one of the first things John had installed. Looking in that direction I was hardly aware that the most distant part of the railroad was only a reflection.

New roadbed board was installed in front of Gorre to provide space for the enginehouse, a couple of yard tracks, and the new mainline tracks.

At the northwest end of the room, to the right of Gorre, there had been a pass-through window from the former dining room to the kitchen. Instead of closing this solidly, John arranged a wallboard backdrop across it, with hinges so the window could be opened for photography or for maintaining hidden tracks.

This end of the layout, containing the original G.D., was completely framed and most roadbed was in place, some without rails. There were several gaps in the terrain. The Great Divide half of the layout had not yet been framed, except for the track along the rear wall. In the large space where framework had not yet been installed, an old dresser was serving as a supply depot for scraps of roadbed material.

John explained that the framework and roadbed were to

climb to Daphetid, then continue on new track down the railroad's steepest grade, 5 percent, to reach a connection with the main line in Great Divide.

A study of his miniature layout models and earliest track plans shows that John had originally intended to model a city in the return loop portion of the small layout—the part that never got built. Now he had more space for the city, and its tall buildings would partly hide the Great Divide yard and spread from there toward the aisleway. Positioning the yard behind other scenery instead of at the front of the layout would prevent the yard from dominating the overall scene.

The city buildings were to be clustered in two groups:

The new mainline tracks in front of Gorre included one spur just above the control panel that was to lead beneath the layout for hidden storage. This feature was never completed, and John never again planned hidden storage tracks.

Great Divide yard on the expanded G.D. was located next to the backdrop, out of reach of the operators, but John never said that it gave them any trouble. The tiny train on the ridge behind the yard was a non-operating scenic detail.

be kept open for as long as possible so he would not have to crawl under the framework. Sometimes his back hurt from stooping.

At Gorre the turntable pit was in place and ties without rails led up to it from several directions. Behind the engine-house was a short length of narrow gauge track and a lone boxcar. It was about three years before that car had any place to go, because the narrow gauge line from Helengon was one of the last things constructed.

The front board between the new control panel and the mainline tracks in front of Gorre was curiously sloped downward. John explained that a track was to go under the layout here, for storage. He never finished this feature.

A small amount of scenic terrain was in place between the old G.D. and the pass-through window. This hid three G.D. mainline tracks beneath it. Above these tracks were the roadbed and ties of the narrow gauge.

I have always been interested in track plans; at one time I could remember every layout I had visited plus most plans published in magazines. John showed me how he planned to develop the remaining parts of the extended G.D. Much of the railroad interest was to be in the front of the layout, where the Austin station would be surrounded by freight facilities and an engine service track.

Though not connected, the Gorre facilities would be adjacent. This device of putting similar things back to back would help create the feeling of a larger railroad while avoiding several separate places cluttered by yards and stations.

To the left of Austin a river and harbor were to be developed. This area was only partly finished when John moved to the Cielo Vista Terrace house in 1953. Further left was Great Divide, with several industrial sidings.

The operating plan was for trains to depart the stub terminal at Great Divide, pass through several intermediate sta-

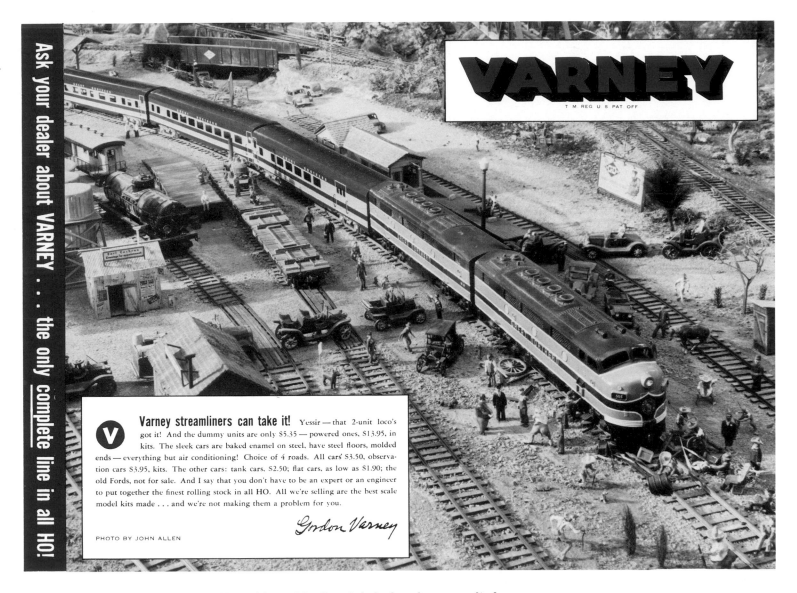

John Allen's name became a household word in model railroad circles largely as a result of a memorable series of advertising photos he took for Gordon Varney of Varney Scale Models. John posed various Varney models on the Gorre & Daphetid, often involving them in eye-catching incidents such as this grade-crossing accident. This particular advertisement was originally featured on the back cover of the November 1953 issue of MODEL RAILROADER.

(Below) Sabotage on the G.D. Line! One of the most momentous events in the first "50 years" of Gorre & Daphetid history was the great pig and cattle car wreck. John staged this sham mishap outside one of the tunnel portals below Daphetid in March 1948.

tions, and reach a return loop after making two laps around the room. From the loop, a cutoff connection would allow trains to run round-and-round laps, if desired, but John said he planned to use that mostly for breaking in locomotives, not operation. He did allow that if trains seemed to get over the line too quickly, he might use the cutoff to have them take an extra lap, but he did not favor that idea.

Operation when I visited was more limited. A train could go from Gorre over the branchline summit to Great Divide. There it could sort cars before continuing on the main line to the end of track in front of Gorre.

The G.D.'s 50th anniversary. —— It was all in fun that John celebrated the 50th anniversary of construction of the Gorre & Daphetid in 1950 when the railroad was actually only 4 years old. "On the G.D. time is 12 times faster than in real life," John explained.

These four photos were all part of the Varney ad campaign. The ads often featured modern equipment that John would not normally operate, such as diesels. The Aerotrain photo (below) is one of the few ad shots made on the last G.D., at the Cielo Vista Terrace house.

On March 11, 1950, John drove the last spike in the main line of the expanded G.D., and shortly afterward he erected a monument to commemorate the occasion. In this photo, looking northwest from Austin, the monument is just below the water tank.

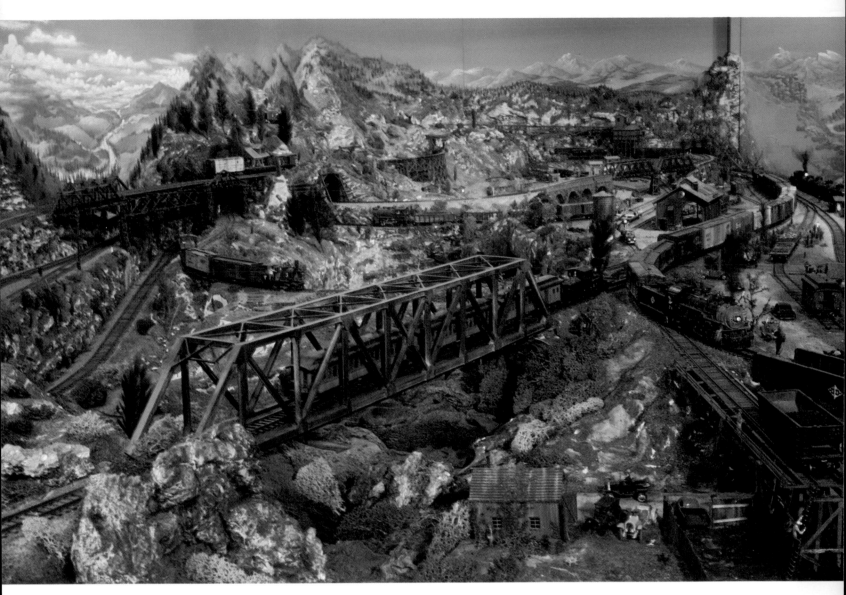

Just before John's second layout was dismantled, the finished areas looked like this. Look carefully and you'll see that the scenery beneath the large truss bridge consists mostly of large rocks and loose lichen tufts positioned temporarily just for this photo.

John prepared an anniversary article in November 1950 and sent it to MODEL RAILROADER. The magazine used the photos and captions in its March 1951 issue, but made no mention of the celebration. The following is from John's original manuscript:

"Since the photo report, MR Jan '48, the Gorre & Daphetid railroad has acquired more territory to serve and has pushed new railroad construction into this area as rapidly as time and resources permit. The original line has become merely a feeder branch connecting to the main line at Great Divide. This original branch line, in turn, receives interchange freight business at Gorre from the three-foot-gauge Devil's Gulch & Helengon RR."

John also wrote that after four years the "long-sought goal" of regular operation had been attained. "Manning the railroad to operate with prototype railroad rules strictly observed needs three engineers, three conductors, and a dispatcher. Frank Ellison's excellent card file system is used."

John reported that on the road's 50th anniversary G.D. Line motive power included six steam locomotives, one gas-electric car, and the president's touring car on railroad wheels. Standard gauge rolling stock was 48 freight cars, three cabooses, four passenger cars, a pay car, and a rotary snowplow. The narrow gauge D.G.& H. had one locomotive, eight freight cars, one caboose, a combination coach-baggage-mail car, and the long "Ruptured Duck" railcar.

At this time the G.D. main line was complete except for about 12 feet of track yet to be laid, and the narrow gauge had 30 of the planned 75 feet of track in place. John estimated it would take three years to complete the scenery.

The Varney ads. —— As the expanded layout neared completion, John took more and more photographs of it. Many of these appeared in articles in MODEL RAILROADER, *Railroad Model Craftsman*, and *HO Model Trains* magazines, but oddly enough, some of his most famous model photos of this

The last trip over the narrow gauge Devil's Gulch & Helengon was, appropriately enough, a railfan excursion. Here it pauses at Helengon yard, in the shadow of Mount Alexander. The automotive contraption on the right was the D.G.& H.'s famous "Ruptured Duck," on which first-class passengers were privileged to ride under the awning.

John hid the right-hand tunnel portal just below Daphetid with a rock, then sprinkled dry texture paint over the layout to make this winter photo for his 1952 Christmas card. He wrote: "I liked it enough to plan a permanent snow area on the new pike."

period appeared not in articles but in some advertisements.

Varney Scale Models of Chicago, Illinois, manufactured one of the largest lines of HO locomotives and cars. Gordon Varney first wrote to John in June 1946 requesting permission to reproduce a photo showing a Varney "Little Joe" Dockside switcher on John's tabletop photo set. John subsequently supplied many more photos, some of them shot to order, and in early 1952 Varney commissioned him to do a series of advertising and catalog photos. Most of these photos appeared as full-page ads on the back cover of MODEL RAILROADER from 1952 to 1959. Each photo showed a scene on the Gorre & Daphetid, including, of course, several Varney products. Gordon Varney himself was both impressed with John's modeling and pleased with the resulting ads. In July 1952 he wrote to John: "I am extremely happy about the way the series is working out. So far, to my mind, the back cover of the MODEL RAILROADER has been better than the front."

The Varney ads often showed rolling stock that John would not normally run on the G.D., among them diesels, streamlined passenger equipment, and the Varney model of the General Motors lightweight Aerotrain. Also included were large doses of the G.D. brand of humor—a diesel salesman lynched from a trestle; shiny diesels in grade crossing collisions with autos and donkey carts; the work dinosaur, Emma, unloading a new Varney diesel power truck; and a score of John's HO people "building" a molded-plastic boxcar. The ads always identified John Allen as the builder of the layout, and this exposure firmly established the G.D. as one of the best-known model railroads in the country.

By 1953 the layout, which by now had been under construction for six years, filled the planned 6½ foot by 20½ foot space. John later wrote that 90 percent of the track and 70 percent of the scenery had been completed. The unfinished areas were those at the left side of the track plan—the city areas of Andrews and Great Divide. The railroad was sufficiently complete for once-a-week operating sessions, which had been going on for some time.

Construction came to a halt early in 1953 when John anticipated a move to new quarters, the Cielo Vista Terrace house. In February he wrote to MODEL RAILROADER editor John Page:

"Since I will be starting my new railroad in 4 or 5 months...I have naturally done considerable planning of the new G.D. Line already, but as time goes along, the details will fall in place. I will be moving into my new house in July or before. There will be quite an area available, perhaps too large for a one-man pike."

House for sale—complete with model railroad. —— As most model railroaders know, moving a layout is not easy. John understood this, and instead of moving the Gorre & Daphetid to Cielo Vista Terrace, he tried to sell the railroad to the new owner of the house. He looked back on what happened in an article written later for the *NMRA Bulletin*:

"Some years ago, 1953 to be exact, when I decided to move, I was confronted with the need to dispose of a former, medium-large G.D. Line three-fourths built. It was built into a house without consideration of construction for later removal. I had already planned a new railroad for a different shape and a larger area in the new house and did not plan to keep the old railroad. It seemed a shame for a good model layout to be wasted though it wasn't one for easy moving. I've never considered model railroads of any commercial value; the time necessary to dismantle about equals the value of the components. I preferred to see the railroad continue to exist, even as a gift.

"In a playful moment I put advertisements in the model magazines offering the pike for sale with house included. The price was set at value of house and property alone. I received lots of letters and distant phone calls requesting information, but as far as I know, no one ever came by for a look at the house. After holding the house for several months, the railroad was torn out and other than some components saved by some friends or myself, the house was sold for a bit more than the original offer to model rails."

Before the G.D. was torn down, John staged a proper fan trip and last run for the camera, and friends even made a motion picture. After the festivities were over, it took the operating crew just two evenings to dismantle the railroad completely. In addition to all rolling stock and bridges, John saved the original 3½ foot by 6½ foot G.D. to be incorporated into his new layout. He gave the beautifully painted linoleum backdrop to one member of the operating crew, the Great Divide classification yard to another friend, and an industrial section of the layout to another. The rest was consigned to the trash can.

John moved into the house on Cielo Vista Terrace in July 1953. These new quarters included a partially excavated basement, and John had already carefully planned the new G.D. to fit into it. Now the stage was set for the great project that was to fill the next 20 years of John Allen's life.

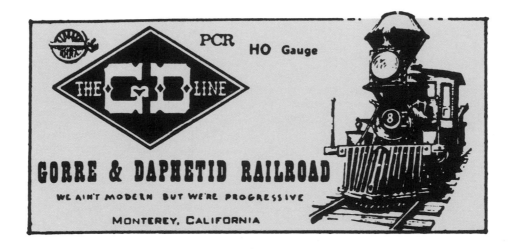

"Right off you might inquire why an individual would build a pike which preferably eight to twelve men should operate. Sometimes I wonder myself. Although the design of the controls is such that one or two men can operate satisfactorily, it is still like driving a bus to go to the store."

Planning the great project

THE HOUSE at 9 Cielo Vista Terrace, Monterey, was not custom built for John, but had been occupied by a family before John purchased it from them. As a result, John had to adapt himself and his model railroad to the requirements imposed by the existing structure, just as most model railroaders must do. There were several months between the time John bought the house and the time he moved in, and he used these months to do extensive planning for the new Gorre & Daphetid.

After John moved in in July 1953, there were many things to be done before railroad construction could commence. The unfinished basement space had to be excavated to full head clearance and concreted, an inside entrance and stairway to the basement built, and electrical outlets and heat installed. These necessary preliminaries gave John, who was a planner by nature, even more time to develop his ideas.

Let's review the layout of the house so as to better understand just what John had to work with, and what he did with it. Remember that the main floor was at street level, but the lot sloped away from the street so steeply that the rear of the main floor had a balcony more than a story above the ground. Below the balcony the foundation wall was a full story high and the basement windows looked down the slope.

Inside the front door was a small square entry. A hallway to the left led past storage closets and the bathroom to the two bedrooms in the north end of the house. The living room was immediately ahead as you entered the front door, and large windows extended across the long rear wall. If you crossed to those windows and turned right you'd find the combined dinette and kitchen, tucked behind the garage.

The narrow stairway to the basement descended from an inconspicuous opening in the living room floor. There was no door at the top of this stairway, and the opening in the floor was protected only by a skimpy railing. John kept a sofa propped against the railing to prevent the staircase from becoming a hazard.

John decided that "about half the 1200 square feet of basement would be allocated for the railroad. The rest would be workshop, photo darkroom, storeroom, and a room for a power saw and lumber storage." Downstairs, under the living room, was to become John's generous workshop, fitted with many shelves and cabinets. The basement area under the bedrooms was originally an unexcavated part of the hill. Here, John dug out most of the earth to make room for the new railroad. He established his photo darkroom in a small room under the kitchen, and a second small room beside the darkroom became a general catchall and a storage area for his cameras.

John built a scale model of the house even before he moved in. This model was a three-layer affair; the roof lifted

This view of the Port industrial complex shows how the alcove looked to a visitor standing in front of the engine terminal at Great Divide. This photo is unusual in that John allowed the mirror between the two tall Port Plastics buildings at right to give itself away by reflecting the upper-tier bridge in front of it.

This is how 9 Cielo Vista Terrace, Monterey, looked when John moved in. Later, because he didn't enjoy yard work, John let the shrubs grow so tall that they almost hid the house.

Here's the future site of the Gorre & Daphetid! We are looking northwest from Port toward Giant Canyon and Devil's Gulch. Most of the basement had to be excavated to full head clearance before John could start work on the railroad. That left ample time for planning.

off to reveal the main floor, which in turn lifted off the foundation so John could study the basement. After deciding how to divide the basement space, John drew rough aisleway boundaries in the railroad area and added black dots to represent the support columns he would have to take into account during track planning.

Now he was ready to begin planning in earnest.

A hobby within a hobby. —— Some model railroaders enjoy planning as much or more than any other aspect of the hobby, and others would rather do a minimum amount of thinking ahead and let projects follow their own course. John was definitely one of the former group—in fact, if anything, he was a "planner's planner." In notes made in 1952 for a book on scenery, he wrote: "Planning can be one of the most enjoyable features of the hobby. Call it armchair railroading if you wish, but it is not idle daydreaming. Whether it be a highly complicated plan or a small portable railroad, it still requires careful planning if the desired result is to be accomplished without unnecessary waste of construction time.

"By 'planning,' I do not limit it to the track plan. I mean planning the framework, wiring, lighting, operation, signalling, types and lengths of trains, type of operation, number of operators desired, as well as scenery planning for variety and eye appeal, and all general planning. Planning is the foundation of your model railroad. It is the most important feature (along with good track)."

Almost 20 years later, John still felt the same way. In an article that was never published, he wrote: "I'm told that there are model railroaders who dislike planning so much that they will do a minimum even though the resulting problems will require much remaking. This is almost inconceivable to me.

"Planning is so pleasurable to me—it's the icing on the cake—that I sometimes feel that to justify the pleasure of long and detailed planning, I must work at constructing the planned feature, if only to find out if the idea was worthwhile. The larger the project, the more possibilities and alternatives can be planned. I've often worked on a series of alternatives for a detailed project that took almost as much

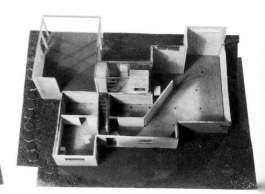

John's planning model of the Cielo Vista house was approximately 6½″ wide by 8½″ long, and came apart in three sections. The small black dots on the basement floor (far right) indicate the locations of support columns. Well-known modeler Paul Jansen took these photos.

John posed this photo to illustrate an article on his ideas about model railroad planning. Although this particular track plan was never built, it does represent an early stage in the development of his plan for the last Gorre & Daphetid layout.

time in planning as the construction of the project itself. Doing so may not get as much railroad built, but the temptations of planning are too much for me to forego this luxury.

"Far from being boring, conceiving an idea and planning it in detail is probably the number one enjoyment of the hobby for me. The interrelationship between requirements and the potential advantages of various solutions gives me great mental stimulus and a great feeling of satisfaction when a problem is solved well."

John's penchant for detailed planning was one of the most remarkable aspects of his remarkable personality, and several of his friends mentioned it when I interviewed them. Alan Fenton, one of the regular G.D. operators, said: "We all knew he only planned one day at a time in his life, but planned many years ahead for his railroad and followed his plan." Cliff Robinson told me: "Everything that he built, he built piece by piece in his mind before he ever started the project. Jim Findley and I are both convinced that his whole railroad was built that way. The wiring was run for everything in advance. He put in wiring in the beginning that

would control a signal he wouldn't install for ten years. A lot of wires were there that were never used."

When I commented to Jim Findley about how John planned everything in advance, Jim replied: "Oh, he was marvelous in that respect, and you appreciated it around the railroad. We were getting ready to install structure lighting at Andrews. I asked him, 'Where are we going to get all those wires? You said you were going to have a night-and-day sequence here, and you were going to pop street lights and house lights and building lights on and off individually in a logical sequence. Where are we going to get all those lines?'

"John answered, 'We put the cable in when we put the cement on the floor.' He had planned all the lighting wiring 16 years before! He detested to go back and do anything a second time. When I built two models of the same small brick station, John looked at me dumbfounded and said, 'You mean you built two of them? Why would you want to build a second one?' "

Criteria for the new layout. —— By the time John moved

CITY CORNER DETAIL WITH MIRROR

into the Cielo Vista Terrace house, he had been an active model railroader for almost eight years. Because he had devoted far more time to the hobby than an average hobbyist, those eight years included a vast amount of model railroad experience. This experience was what molded the criteria for the new layout.

Writing later on concept and planning of the G.D., John was almost certainly referring to his first two layouts when he said, "Unfortunately the model railroad builder needs the most experience and knowledge before he starts planning and building. He is likely to end up with the wrong railroad because his concept and desires are almost certain to change as he gains operating experience. The concept and operating scheme are the essence of a model railroad. The track plan is merely a method to attain that end. Unfortunately, most model railroads seem to be designed in reverse order."

The new G.D. would have a strong concept and operating scheme, and its track plan would be designed for prototypical operation and spectacular scenic effect. John made up a list of factors to be considered in planning a layout:

- Time available for construction
- Permanence of location
- Money and space available
- Operating preferences
- How many will operate
- Construction desires
- Equipment preferences
- Features you enjoy most and wish to emphasize

Let's examine how John dealt with each of these factors as he planned the new G.D. Line.

By 1953 John's investments had appreciated greatly, and he could afford to be very selective about the advertising photography assignments he accepted. While he had many other interests to keep him busy, he had almost unlimited time available for construction. Even so, he expected the new layout would take 20 years to complete.

John did not have to worry about changing houses due to family pressures or a job shift, so he could design and build the layout in the expectation it would never have to be moved. Money was not a problem either, but not for the reason you might think. John always preferred "to build rather than buy ready-made," so his modeling required only modest expenditures for materials.

After excavation, the total space available in the basement was approximately 1200 square feet. As we have al-

(Above) John's notebooks were filled with detailed planning sketches like this one. (Below) Note how closely this 1968 color photo of Great Divide yard and Cross Junction matches John's March 1954 sketch.

ready seen, John elected to use only half of that for the railroad. Years later he admitted privately that he would not undertake such a large project if he had it to do again, mainly because in later years the railroad required considerable maintenance to keep it running well.

John had strong, well-defined operating preferences by 1953, and these preferences continued to develop during construction of the new layout. In 1965, in notes for a book on the Gorre & Daphetid, he wrote, "I believe a model railroad should be more than a miniature scene to store a collection of model railroad equipment or merely a place to allow that equipment to exercise. It should be planned and constructed for model operation, for otherwise it is like a museum, or a stage set without any play."

These operating preferences included the challenges of mainline mountain railroading—single track, steep grades, short trains, and helper service—and "the dovetailing of operation and dispatching required when many crews are working." After long and thoughtful consideration, John decided to make the G.D. represent only a single division of a railroad crossing a rugged mountain range. Its operation would ultimately include through freights running across the division, through passenger service, local passenger trains, and local peddler freights. The single big yard facility at Great Divide would allow some classification switching, but such switching was not one of John's strong operational preferences. For him, the real action took place out on the main line.

How many operators would it take to keep the trains moving? Three or four, at least, and more as the layout neared completion and the full complexity of operation became possible. Why would a bachelor, living alone, want to build such a layout? "I live in an area where a great many military personnel, both Army and Navy, are stationed. This type of modeler must move regularly, and for them, anything larger than a portable railroad is almost out of the question. Many model railroaders are in the services, so a club type railroad designed for many operators would benefit them. Since I prefer multiple-crew operation anyway, I decided to build this type of railroad."

John's construction desires were closely related to his emphasis on operation and his enjoyment of all phases of layout construction. They were also quite realistic. He realized that in building so large a layout he could not possibly work in sequence, building all the benchwork, then laying all the track, then completing the wiring, and so on, before starting the scenery—and more important, commencing operation. "One requirement I insisted upon in the track plan was that after not more than one-fourth of the track was constructed, a good way freight operation could be run. This is necessary to prevent pushing construction too fast, which may result in sloppy workmanship. This is supposed to be a hobby for pleasure, and getting bored with too much repetition in construction work is a good way to sour the enthusiasm."

John was equally realistic about the locomotives and cars he planned to operate on the new Gorre & Daphetid. "Equipment preferences can be a booby trap if you, as I do, like all varieties and eras. If you include all types of equipment, your pike is likely to end up looking more like a museum than a working railroad. Each modeler will have to solve this for himself. It becomes more difficult for a club railroad. It often requires much soul searching. For instance, I like massive modern steam power, yet restrained myself to conform to my railroad concept and built a railroad on which massive steam power can't be used. To assure that later I wouldn't renege, I built the turntable too short and the clearances on embankments and tunnel portals too close for large power. This wasn't done lightly."

The last factor on John's list was "Features you enjoy most and wish to emphasize." For the new G.D. these features could very nearly be summed up in two words: "mountain railroading." John liked everything about mountain railroads, the twisting track, steep grades, short trains and high proportion of locomotives to cars, low speeds, and spectacular scenic possibilities. Perhaps most of all he liked bridges: "A mountain railroad won't suit you if you don't like to build bridges. Bridges come in droves in the mountains...Since I like bridge research and bridge construction, the need for so many of them on a mountain line was an incentive rather than a dissuasion...The new G.D. Line is defi-

Compare this 1956 photo of the location of Scalp Mountain with the view showing the unexcavated basement (page 76). This area was only partially dug out, then Squawbottom Creek and Devil's Gulch were roughly modeled into the poured concrete.

nitely a mountain railroad, with steep grades, sharp curves, and a good number and variety of bridges."

John had planned to include city scenes on his earlier layouts, and cityscape would be prominent on the new G.D.: "Since one of my principal interests is industrial switching, about one-third of the area of the layout is not in the rugged mountains. There are, or will be, about 40 industries in this third of the railroad, and less than 20 industries in the mountainous two-thirds."

Developing the track plan. —— As early as 1950, John began sketching track plans for a larger model railroad. Because most of these plans were far too large to fit into the little house on Irving Street and far too detailed to be passed off as idle doodling, John was already toying with the idea of moving to larger quarters.

John drew one or more new track plans each month from September 1950 until June 1952. These plans started out modest enough, but gradually they became more and more like the new G.D. Line. The plan dated March 1952 is the first to show the original little G.D. incorporated into the larger layout. The last dated sketch of this period was done in June 1952. In December John drew the first sketch showing how this layout would fit into the basement of the Cielo Vista Terrace house. By June 1953, a month before he moved in, the basic shape of the layout was firmly established. By November 1953 John had all but finalized the plan, and he made several 8"x 10" photographic prints on which he sketched in details and added notes on the back. Much of this detailed planning would not be realized for 15 years, but it was all conceived months before the first stick of wood was sawn.

When John drew the final plan he had settled on the following features:

●A walk-in, around-the-walls layout arrangement, with the railroad against the walls and access aisles reaching into the layout area. John added a peninsula jutting into the center of

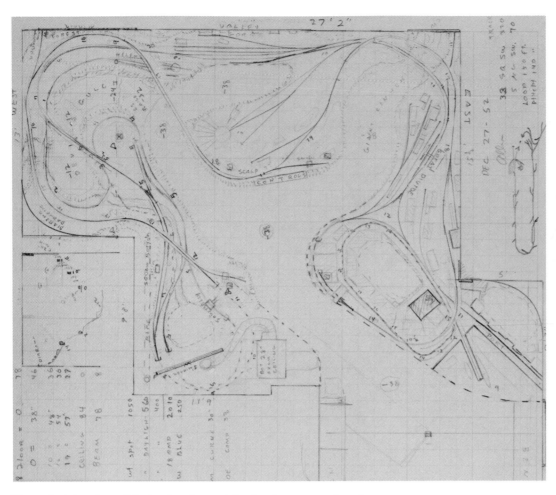

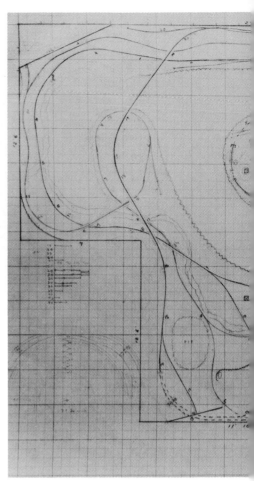

These sketches from John's planning notebooks show some steps in the evolution of the final Gorre & Daphetid track plan. The December 1952 sketch (above) has the same overall configuration as the eventual layout, but the main line only goes around the room twice. The November 1953 plan (center) is the one John made several photographic prints of for additional detailed planning. It differs from the layout as built chiefly in the arrangement of tracks at Sims Loop, Squawbottom, and Akin. John drew the final plan (far right) after the railroad had already been under construction for several years.

the room to accommodate the portion of the old layout. Early sketches show that John had worked with the idea of an isolated operating pit, but later discarded it. No duck unders or pop-up holes would be required for access to the railroad during normal operation.

●A point-to-point operating scheme with provisions for alternate routings, especially until the main line was completed.

●Dramatic mountain railroading, with great vertical separation between tracks, scenery to the floor, and considerable track at or above eye level. John wrote that "the nearer a model pike got up to eye level, the larger and better it looked...Without doubt, visually the largest possible pike that could be built in a given area would be a railroad built along the side of a steep mountainside in rugged country. Scenery could go from ceiling to floor and trains would start at or near floor level, and by travelling around the side of the mountain, up steep grades, could finally rise above eye height or even to the ceiling."

●A single-track main line, without the appearance of dou-

ble track where two tracks were close together: "Tracks near each other but at different levels always appear further removed than if they are at the same elevation. This effect is not readily apparent on a track plan, but can be depended upon when viewed on the layout. Even a few scale feet in elevation helps disassociate the tracks visually."

●Significant city areas for industrial switching, including a waterfront with a car ferry and real water. John later wrote: "Visually, all of the city area is one, but schematically that at higher elevation is Great Divide while Port is below...grouping cities together keeps the country area free and enhances both from a visual standpoint."

●A narrow gauge feeder, but less extensive than the Devil's Gulch & Helengon on the expanded layout at Irving Street.

Operating schemes. —— On the final track plan, the main line has two subdivisions: the "summit" line from Great Divide to Port, using the two upper tiers of the layout; and the "river" line from Port to Gorre, using the two lower tiers. A good way to remember how the track plan works is that for westbound movements (from Great Divide to Gorre) each subdivision first runs counterclockwise along the east, north, and west walls of the room to a turnback curve at Helengon Gap in the south alcove. The return trip is clockwise along the same walls, but on the next lower tier. Each transit of the main line is at the next lower elevation until reaching the low point at Squawbottom. The main line then climbs back up to the western terminal at Gorre. (Schematic A)

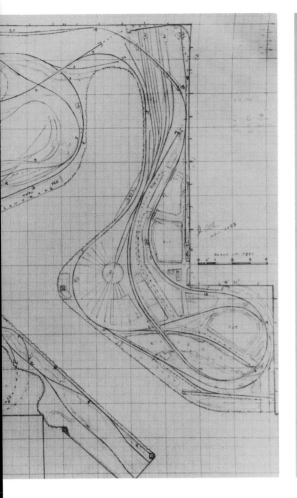

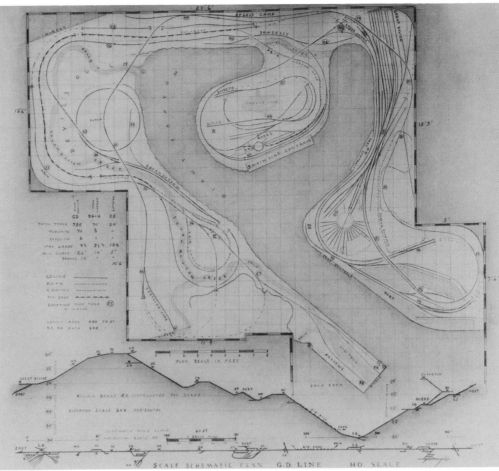

The track that continues beyond Gorre, past Devil's Post Pile and over Ryan Trestle, is the cutoff route back to Great Divide. Though not a part of the ultimate point-to-point concept, the cutoff allows a number of special routings and alternate operating schemes:

• It is possible to run out to Gorre over the mainline route, then use the cutoff as far as Cross Junction to loop back over most of the same route (except for Sowbelly and Squawbottom) to Great Divide. This is "out-and-back," or "point-to-loop-and-back." (Schematic B)

• It is possible to repeat the entire mainline run in continuous fashion. Trains reaching Gorre over the point-to-point mainline route can continue over the cutoff and rejoin the main line at the cutoff switch in Great Divide, making any number of laps. Continuous running is possible in either direction. (Schematic C)

• By using the return loop options at Port and Cross Junction, point-to-loop operation becomes possible. Trains run through Port on their first trip over the layout, then terminate there after their second traverse of the main line. (Schematic D)

• If trains depart Great Divide via the cutoff and proceed to Gorre, the main line becomes the eastbound route between Great Divide and Port. Port serves as the terminal for over-the-line movements, and the two summit subdivision segments between Port and Cold Shoulder and Great Divide and Angels Camp become branchline operations. Because John never completed the great bridge between Scalp Mountain

This G.D. train climbing out of the Helengon alcove on the rugged 3.5 percent grade up to Port illustrates John's principle of separating tracks vertically. Squawbottom siding, at lower right, is just a few inches away, but the slight difference in elevation effectively separates the tracks much more for the viewer.

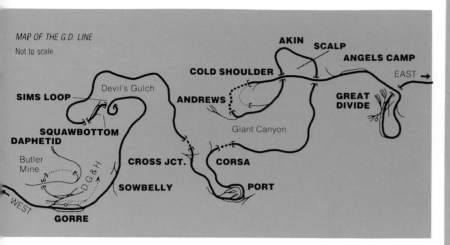

MAP OF THE G.D. LINE
Not to scale

This is how John fitted his concept of the G.D. as a single mountain division of a larger railroad onto an idealized topographic map of the Akinbak region. Trains would roll west from Great Divide, over the summit at Scalp and Cold Shoulder, through Port, through Devil's Gulch, and depart the division westbound from Gorre.

To ensure that it would not dominate the layout, John placed the Great Divide classification yard in the northeast corner of the railroad room. This was one of the first areas he built.

and Angels Camp, this temporary routing was the one most often used to operate the railroad. (Schematic E)

•The cutoff will allow engines to run between Port, Gorre, and the main engine facility at Great Divide without going over miles of main line. This feature makes it unnecessary to crowd the layout with additional large, space-consuming engine facilities.

•At Great Divide, Gorre, and Cross Junction, the cutoff trackage can represent interchange tracks with connecting railroads.

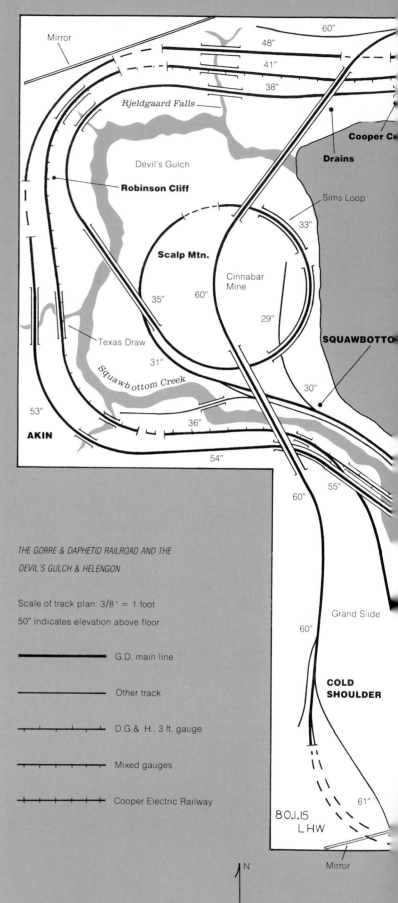

THE GORRE & DAPHETID RAILROAD AND THE
DEVIL'S GULCH & HELENGON

Scale of track plan: 3/8″ = 1 foot
50″ indicates elevation above floor

—————————— G.D. main line

—————————— Other track

—+—+—+—+— D.G.& H., 3 ft. gauge

—+—+—+—+— Mixed gauges

—+—+—+—+— Cooper Electric Railway

80.1.15
LHW

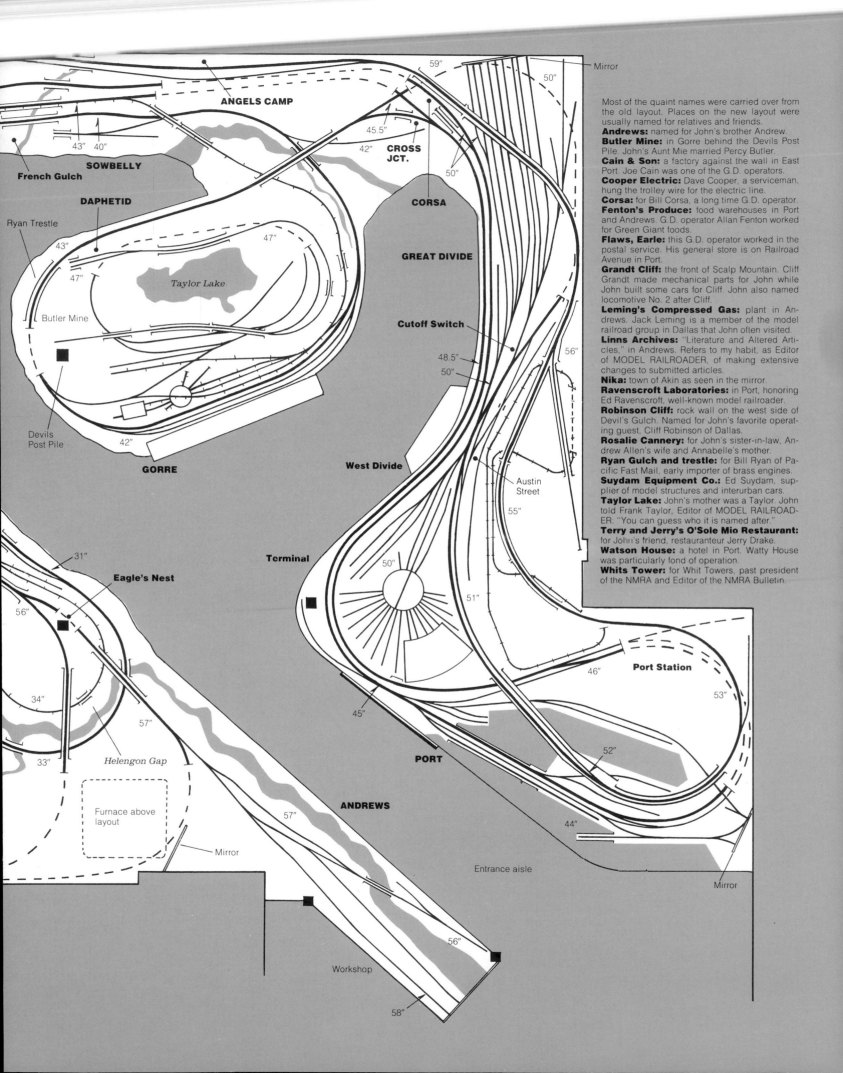

ANGELS CAMP

59"

50"

Mirror

45.5"

42"

CROSS
JCT.

50"

SOWBELLY

French Gulch

43" 40"

DAPHETID

CORSA

Ryan Trestle

43"

47"

GREAT DIVIDE

47"

Taylor Lake

Cutoff Switch

Butler Mine

56"

48.5"

50"

Devils
Post Pile

42"

West Divide

GORRE

Austin
Street

55"

31"

Terminal

50"

Eagle's Nest

56"

51"

34"

Port Station

53"

57"

46"

Helengon Gap

33"

*Furnace above
layout*

PORT

52"

Mirror

ANDREWS

57"

44"

Entrance aisle

Mirror

Workshop

56"

58"

Most of the quaint names were carried over from the old layout. Places on the new layout were usually named for relatives and friends.

Andrews: named for John's brother Andrew.

Butler Mine: in Gorre behind the Devils Post Pile. John's Aunt Mie married Percy Butler.

Cain & Son: a factory against the wall in East Port. Joe Cain was one of the G.D. operators.

Cooper Electric: Dave Cooper, a serviceman, hung the trolley wire for the electric line.

Corsa: for Bill Corsa, a long time G.D. operator.

Fenton's Produce: food warehouses in Port and Andrews. G.D. operator Allan Fenton worked for Green Giant foods.

Flaws, Earle: this G.D. operator worked in the postal service. His general store is on Railroad Avenue in Port.

Grandt Cliff: the front of Scalp Mountain. Cliff Grandt made mechanical parts for John while John built some cars for Cliff. John also named locomotive No. 2 after Cliff.

Leming's Compressed Gas: plant in Andrews. Jack Leming is a member of the model railroad group in Dallas that John often visited.

Linns Archives: "Literature and Altered Articles," in Andrews. Refers to my habit, as Editor of MODEL RAILROADER, of making extensive changes to submitted articles.

Nika: town of Akin as seen in the mirror.

Ravenscroft Laboratories: in Port, honoring Ed Ravenscroft, well-known model railroader.

Robinson Cliff: rock wall on the west side of Devil's Gulch. Named for John's favorite operating guest, Cliff Robinson of Dallas.

Rosalie Cannery: for John's sister-in-law, Andrew Allen's wife and Annabelle's mother.

Ryan Gulch and trestle: for Bill Ryan of Pacific Fast Mail, early importer of brass engines.

Suydam Equipment Co.: Ed Suydam, supplier of model structures and interurban cars.

Taylor Lake: John's mother was a Taylor. John told Frank Taylor, Editor of MODEL RAILROADER: "You can guess who it is named after."

Terry and Jerry's O'Sole Mio Restaurant: for John's friend, restauranteur Jerry Drake.

Watson House: a hotel in Port. Watty House was particularly fond of operation.

Whits Tower: for Whit Towers, past president of the NMRA and Editor of the NMRA Bulletin.

The Gorre & Daphetid passenger terminal and office building dominated the yard scene at Great Divide. Look carefully and you'll see
where the mirror surface touches the roof of the pedestrian overpass.

Design and operating problems. —— The most important
terminal is Great Divide. One of the problems in designing a
model railroad is that main terminal yards can dominate the
space, making the rest of the railroad look small. John handled this problem by, in a sense, hiding Great Divide in a corner. The yard is located where, most of the time, it is behind a
viewer's back as he looks at the rest of the railroad. This way,
Great Divide cannot dominate the overall scene.

John further deemphasized Great Divide by designing it
as a stub, rather than double-ended or through, terminal. By
doing so he made a great savings in the space necessary for
the yard, and introduced operating complexities that he
liked: "I prefer a stub terminal with a turntable for turning
trains, and this includes some passenger cars on my line."

He included other built-in operating problems as well: "In
track design my thoughts are not to plan extra track to make
operation too easy. Too many loops, wye tracks and runaround sidings can take a lot of the head work out of operation. G.D. way freights always work all spurs, both facing-
point and trailing-point, and some of these are blind from the

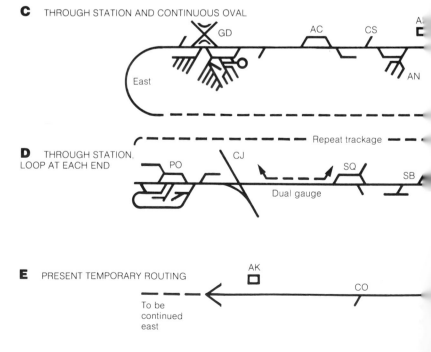

engineer's cab so the engineer must be directed by hand signals from a conductor or flagman. The spur tracks at Sowbelly are directly off the main line; there is no runaround and the operator cannot see from his cab unless he is at least 6'-3" tall. It is a problem for the dispatcher as well as the train crew, but we like it fine."

The single greatest designed-in operating problem on the Gorre & Daphetid, however, was that of any mountain railroad: grades. Determined by careful measurement of the track plan, the average grade of the G.D. main line is 2.5 percent, but John considered the line equivalent to a 4 percent grade because of the increased friction that occurs when a train already on a grade encounters sharp curves. In addition, John differentiated between maximum and ruling grades: "My standard gauge has a higher maximum grade than ruling grade because I follow the prototype practice of using a steeper grade at the start of a grade, where part of the train is still on level track. Then the grade eases below the

ruling percent to allow the engine to keep its footing as the whole train gets onto the grade."

By John's measurement the track plan included 720 feet of track, with 370 feet of main line. The minimum radius on the main line was 26" (at Sims Loop), with a branchline minimum radius of 14" (on the portion of the old layout that was saved). There were 14 tunnels, six passing sidings from 6½ to 13 feet long, and ten towns. The abbreviated narrow gauge was to have 70 feet of track, 33 feet of it dual gauge, a minimum radius of 17", and a maximum grade of 3.5 percent. John calculated that the layout occupied about 430 of the available 630 square feet, with the rest occupied by aisles.

The miniature layout. —— John's final step in planning the new layout was to construct a miniature model. "If you are planning a pike that is going to take several years to construct, why not spend a little time building a miniature model of the proposed railroad? I certainly recommend it. It

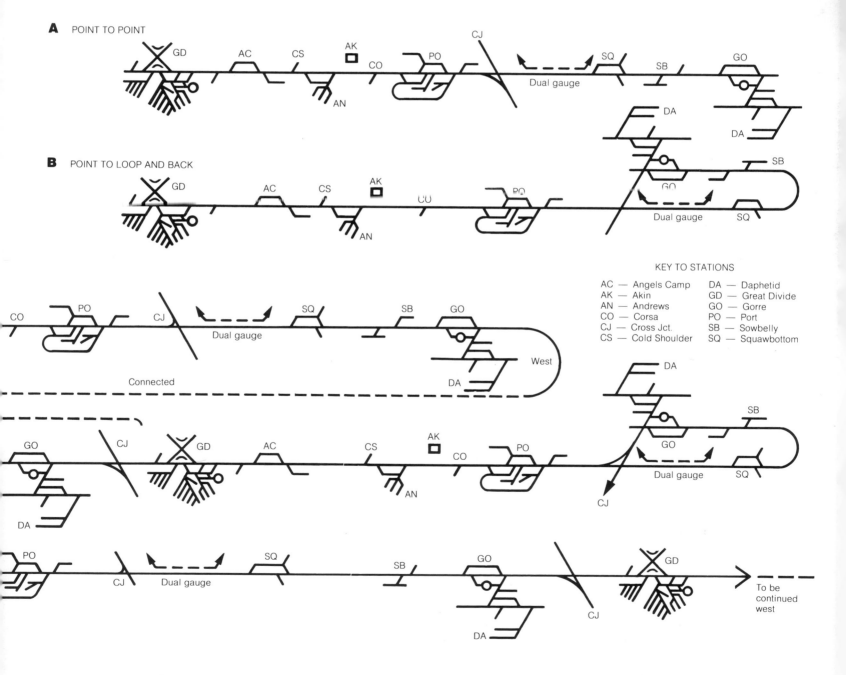

KEY TO STATIONS

AC — Angels Camp   DA — Daphetid
AK — Akin   GD — Great Divide
AN — Andrews   GO — Gorre
CO — Corsa   PO — Port
CJ — Cross Jct.   SB — Sowbelly
CS — Cold Shoulder SQ — Squawbottom

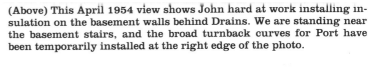

(Above) This April 1954 view shows John hard at work installing insulation on the basement walls behind Drains. We are standing near the basement stairs, and the broad turnback curves for Port have been temporarily installed at the right edge of the photo.

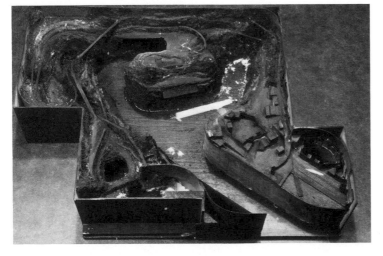

The upper photo of this pair shows how John built miniature layout models. After adding cardboard roadbed to a plywood base, he built up scenery with modeling clay. The bottom photo is his 12″ by 16″ model based on the December 1952 plan. Although the track changed considerably, the basic shape remained about the same.

(Left) Already 192 feet above Squawbottom Creek and still climbing the stiff grade toward Cold Shoulder, a special old-time excursion train crosses Squaw Creek High Bridge. Just out of the photo to the right is Eagle's Nest, where the train will pause while the passengers detrain for a meal at the top-of-the-mountain restaurant.

will point out mistakes not readily noticed in a flat plan. It can be changed in very little time, and in the long run I am sure will actually save overall construction time as well as clarify your mind as to just how high and steep that hill should be, where it is most logical to put the bridge over the river, and so forth. The model can be as carefully detailed or as lacking in details as you desire. However, be sure to keep it to exact scale. Plot your track curves accurately, and make elevations correct.

"A small railroad could be modeled at a scale of 1½″ to the foot, a medium-size pike 1″ scale, large railroads ¾″ equals a foot, and extra-large or club pikes, ⅜″ to the foot. It's best to draw up a scale rule in scale inches and feet on a strip of cardboard or celluloid to use to transfer dimensions from the track plan. I like to cut all curves out of cardboard on which the track has been drawn to scale radii so I know the curves will not be distorted on the finished model. Hills can be added with modeling clay—gray-green or brown looks best—which allows changes to be made easily.

"It's entirely unnecessary to make a highly detailed model, but it is a lot of fun and will show you how the final layout will look. The clay can be painted by giving it a flat coat of white shoe milk and then painting with ordinary poster paint. This will be very helpful in deciding color later on. You will find you will consult this plan over and over during pike construction, and if basic or minor changes of the plan are contemplated, a change in the model will help decide and save a great deal of time. You'll be surprised how many good ideas will come to you about improving the original plan, particularly in regard to scenery."

In 1967 I asked John to write an article on what he would do differently if he were to design the Gorre & Daphetid over again. He replied in a letter: "For the time being, I'd rather not do the article, principally because my ideas might change farther and also because few people really know what I am doing now. But the principal change would be that I would not bite off such a large project. As I grow older I produce less, and the unfinished portion of the layout looms ever larger. It is easy to plan, but more difficult to accomplish."

"Construction still has a long way to go. There is no schedule for building, but it was originally estimated that it would take about 20 years for the layout to be basically completed, if ever...As each new spur or addition of track is completed, it is incorporated into the operation. About 60 feet of main line remains to be constructed. It may be years before it is."

Building the empire

CONSTRUCTION of the new Gorre & Daphetid began in January 1954. While there isn't room to describe how John built each and every detail of the new railroad, I'll point out some of his most interesting techniques, especially those devices he used to make the railroad seem larger than it was. I'll also try, in a general way, to chronicle John's progress toward realizing his comprehensive plan for the layout.

John's first order of business in 1953 was to excavate the basement to full head clearance. In 1961 he wrote: "Since basic planning preceded excavation, I found that one area need not be dug out. When this earth was roughly contoured and three inches of rough concrete modeled over it, it would form a canyon bottom (Devil's Gulch) which could be walked upon for access."

After the concrete came an inside stairway, electrical out-

We're standing beside the Devils Post Pile, watching an eastbound Gorre & Daphetid log train proceed slowly over Ryan Trestle. Just to the right of the train is the stub end of the Daphetid Branch, and high above is the tiny wild-west town of Angels Camp.

By July 1954 the basement at 9 Cielo Vista Terrace looked like this. The uppermost tier of roadbed, the summit line to Angels Camp, is in place against the wall behind Sowbelly, and John has started to build new scenery between Sowbelly and Cross Junction.

lets, and heat. Three support posts, including one near the passenger station at Great Divide and one at the future site of Scalp Mountain, were removed after some of the floor beams were strengthened. The diagonal braces between the support posts were also removed.

John insulated the outside walls, covering the basement windows: "No windows were desired in the railroad area, so that lighting could be controlled during the day as well as at night." Using the miniature model of the railroad to aid in planning, John installed lighting, including blue bulbs for the night effect that had been a feature of the previous G.D. Several years later he added the mechanism for a gradual (8- to 10-minute) transition between day and night.

Lighting—4000 watts worth. —— As he did on so many other topics, John had strong opinions about lighting: "Lighting is an important but much-neglected feature of model railroads. Often it is only an afterthought, and then it may be very difficult to install properly. Plan the lighting from the first, decide the type of lighting most suited for your style of pike, and if possible install it early so as to get the benefit of adequate light during construction, as well as to better judge the scenery painting to blend in with the shadows."

Of lighting the new G.D., John wrote: "This road is one of the most difficult types to light because the 7-foot ceiling is only 2 feet above some trackage. Also, because of the walk-in feature it is difficult to arrange lights so a viewer need not look into bulbs. An 8″ valance drops from the ceiling to shield most bulbs; shades are used to hide others.

"Lights are a combination of 150-watt spotlights that simulate warm, directional sunlight filtering down through the clouds, and numerous smaller tungsten 'daylight' bulbs that simulate cool blue reflective fill from the sky. Fluorescent lamps are not used, because the simpler kinds cannot be dimmed to zero for the transitional day-to-night effect. A night lighting system coordinates with the day circuits. All in all, the lighting totals about 4000 watts, and average intensity is about 1 candlepower per square foot. Color balance is for type B Ektachrome film without a filter."

On the subject of lighting for photos, John wrote to me in 1968: "My photos, with few exceptions, are shot under room lights without added supplements. They are really records, without intent to fake or augment. I try to get atmosphere into the distant parts of a scene by painting and lighting them with blued hues and colors close in value as are found in nature. When I shoot a distant scene it naturally will be grayed and less contrasty than a nearby scene."

The unusual vertical lift at Port allowed access for routine maintenance by sending a cluster of the city structures skyward. The platform had a vertical wood rail on each side, and could be locked in the raised position. This 1968 view shows John hard at work.

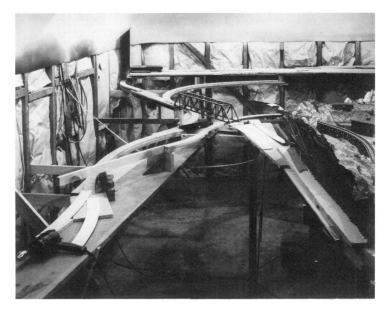

This June 1954 view looking toward Great Divide is one of the earliest G.D. construction photos. The portion saved from the old railroad is on the right, and we can see the edge of the Great Divide mirror and the roadbed for the cutoff line running behind and beneath it.

John's smooth hand-laid trackwork was one of the G.D. Line's greatest assets. This construction view of the classification yard throat and ladder at Great Divide shows how John fitted the turnouts close together so he could squeeze in at least one additional track.

This hinged panel below Cold Shoulder, an area called Grand Slide, provided access for maintenance work in the Helengon Gap alcove. The incomplete roadbed of the D.G.& H. narrow gauge is just across Squawbottom Creek from the G.D. main line here.

Here's John's friend Jim Findley in the access hole at Great Divide yard. Jim's reflection destroys the mirror illusion and shows why John stressed placing and orienting the mirrors in such a way that non-railroad objects could never be seen in them.

Next came the backdrop: "The backdrop is linoleum, painted with sky, clouds, and some distant ground. The bottom of the backdrop is normal eye level, and all scenery or buildings must overlap this line." After putting up the linoleum, gently curving it in the corners of the room, John painted it plain, uniform blue down to the horizon line. Later, as portions of the layout approached completion, he went back and added clouds, smoke, and scenic grandeur. During this finish painting he also painted out shadows on the backdrop.

John enjoyed experimenting with special background effects. He added dramatic smoke and smog over the cityscape at Port and Great Divide, and poised a thunderstorm over Cross Junction, an effect he later undid. He compounded the trickery in one instance by photographing the model buildings at Port, coloring the photo, and using it behind the buildings at Austin.

Benchwork, rail, and track. —— By April 1954 John had erected benchwork for Great Divide yard, Great Divide engine terminal, and the projecting peninsula that would support the portion of the old layout that he had saved. Wherever possible he anchored the railroad to the walls and support posts, adding 2 x 4 legs only where necessary.

John used laminated roadbed consisting of ¾" plywood with ½" Homasote, a dense composite material made from used newsprint, or Firtex, a similar product made from wood fibers, glued on top. These materials were chosen for their sound-deadening properties and their ability to take and hold spikes. Because he had planned so carefully in advance, John was able to cut most of the curved roadbed sections at one time. He used a homemade template to shape transition spirals at each end of the curves, and fitted straight sections between the curves later, on the layout.

Track for the G.D. was all hand-laid, with the exception of a few sections of commercial flexible track installed in the hidden curves near Cold Shoulder. "I cut my own ties out of wood on a saw, stain them to a weathered color, and glue them in place, dropping rock ballast (sand) in place over the same wet glue. After the glue hardens the excess ballast is removed with a vacuum cleaner and the rail is then spiked in place...Once you know how to build trackwork you don't have to conform to only the track available." From the beginning, John had few derailments due to misaligned track.

John hand-laid his track because he wanted realistic scale appearance, something that wasn't a feature of the commercial trackwork then available. Even before he started the new layout he had tried to get the NMRA interested in encouraging smaller rail for HO than the then-standard code 100 ("code" is the actual height of the rail in thousandths of an inch), which was larger than that used by even the heaviest prototype railroads. In 1962 he wrote: "My largest mainline rail is some British code 88 that I bought some years ago before we had nickel silver rail over here. Only my trolley line, where the rail is hidden in the pavement, and the old original branch line [to Daphetid] have rail as large as code 100. All is nickel silver, except for some brass installed in a few short lengths only to see how it performs. About 60 percent of my track is code 70, but I also use a considerable amount of British code 65. It cannot be spiked, so I use contact cement under it. It is used for narrow gauge and some standard gauge spurs."

Mainline curves on the G.D. were superelevated, that is, the outer rail was made higher than the inner one as is done on prototype railroads. This is a subject of great debate among model railroaders, some arguing that it is unnecessary and detrimental to good operation, and others agreeing with John: "I have never considered superelevation a me-

Here's another candid portrait of Jim Findley, this time posed in the access opening behind Austin Street suburban station. This access was simply an open hole behind the structures in this part of the sprawling Great Divide and Port cityscape.

chanically needed feature, but rather one to improve prototype appearance of track and trains. The appearance of a model train leaning into a curve is a beautiful sight that gives the cars the appearance of heft and weight. I don't believe a scale 5" or 6" is needed or desirable, but a scale 2½" or about ¹/₃₂" is a big help in appearance. It will cause no trouble if the approaches to the curves are smooth. I consider superelevation just as necessary as the many other details we model that have no mechanical need, such as valve gear, brake wheels, rivets, and so forth."

Making the railroad accessible. —— Most of the new layout would be accessible from the walk-in aisles, but several areas required special provisions for construction and maintenance. John's access criteria, based on his height (6 feet) were as follows: "I take it as a rule in my planning to have nothing over a 3-foot reach, no track more than 2'-6", and no turnouts, crossings, or movable uncoupling ramps more than 2 feet due to difficulty in maintenance." He recommended adding or subtracting ½" from each of these dimensions for each inch you are taller or shorter than 6 feet.

Perhaps the most ingenious access was at Port, where John built a vertical lift hatch. This consisted of a horizontal cover resting on two vertical side rails that slid up and down in guides mounted in the layout. The hatch was covered with structures, and to use the access John raised the lift until the structures almost touched the ceiling, locked it into position, and stood in the resulting hole.

Another access opening was located among the structures behind Austin Street station in Great Divide, and there was a lift-out hatch in the middle of Great Divide passenger terminal. Although this was the only hatch that carried track, John said he never had problems with derailments here.

A large section of removable scenery just to the west of Cross Junction provided access to two stretches of hidden track and the Sowbelly Creek area. Further west, the concrete walkway up Devil's Gulch was the means of reaching the track along Robinson Cliff, the back side of Scalp Mountain, and the remote town of Akin.

Access to Helengon Gap, the deep alcove behind Eagle's Nest, was via an ingenious trapdoor hinged at its upper edge, like a drop leaf on a dining table. The hinged edge was just below snowy Cold Shoulder, in an area called Grand Slide. Some of John's most dramatic photos of trains on the high bridge approaching Eagle's Nest were taken from here. Finally, the hidden turnback curves deep in Helengon Gap could be reached from underneath the scenery.

Making the most of the space. —— Even though the new G.D. was more than three times as large as the old, John used every trick in his arsenal to make the railroad seem even larger than it was. We've already learned how he planned to use vertical space by running track from only 30" from floor level at Squawbottom almost to the ceiling at Angels Camp, and by increasing the visible surface area with skyscrapers, gorges, and soaring mountain peaks. John further expanded the horizons of the G.D. through the clever use of mirrors, by modeling some areas in reduced scale, and by cleverly disguising obstacles.

"Mirrors can open a wall and increase the apparent size of a room if used correctly," John wrote in 1961. "I plan to use four; two are now in place." By 1972, John had far exceeded his original estimate, and there were over 30 mirrors on the layout! The first mirror on the new G.D. was at Great Divide passenger terminal. Angled slightly away from the wall so it wouldn't reflect visitors or non-railroad features, it effectively doubled the apparent length of the yard tracks.

"The mirrors usually are not noticed right away, but they seem to bring a ripple of excitement when the feature is realized," John said. The largest mirror, second to be installed, was in the northwest corner of the room, above Devil's Gulch. It was 6 feet wide and 2 feet high. Depending upon where the viewer or camera was located, this mirror reflected the burned-over forest in front of it, the back of Scalp Mountain, the Devil's Post Pile, or the town of Akin (the reflection, appropriately, was dubbed "Nika"—Akin spelled backwards).

Two more large mirrors were eventually located on the layout, one in Helengon Gap behind Cold Shoulder, and one at Andrews. Among the numerous small mirrors were those located inside the subway at Port and the parking lot under Great Divide engine terminal, several inside the Compressed Space factory at Andrews, one between the old and new Port Plastics buildings, and another where the Cooper Electric trolley line disappeared under a building in Port. This last mirror provided the illusion that the trolley line ran straight ahead, when in reality it turned sharply to the left, back toward the Austin Street suburban station.

John employed reduced-scale modeling to make the most of several cramped spaces. "When your layout is against a wall, the space beyond the last visible track can be used very effectively to help enlarge the appearance of the scene. This forced perspective starts with full-scale buildings or scenery next to the track, reducing the scale as the perspective recedes until the modeling is at a much-reduced scale. The backdrop painting continues the scene." He applied this diorama technique to the tiny towns of Akin and Angels Camp, both of which were near eye level.

John removed three of the support posts in the railroad room, but he was left with three posts and two room corners jutting into the space. Two of the posts became towering rock pinnacles, Devils Post Pile and Eagle's Nest, and John planned to hide the post near Great Divide engine terminal with a tall grain elevator.

Of the corners at Port and Andrews, John said: "I try to make any room obstruction appear as though it is a desired feature rather than ignore it or hide it apologetically. Corners jutting out into a room can be difficult to hide. I have two of these protruding corners; one is disguised by a high mountainside [at Andrews], and the other has the railroad's tallest building rising up to touch the ceiling. It may not make the corner into an asset, but it helps hide the offending projection and takes very little plan space."

Highball westward! —— By July 1954 John was making rapid progress. He installed the portion saved from the old layout, then added the scenery around it, including Devils Post Pile. By July 1955 tracks extended out of Gorre, through Cross Junction, and into Great Divide. Photos taken in August 1956 show track reaching into Port, control panels installed at Gorre, Great Divide, and Port, Great Divide yard virtually complete except for the engine terminal, and benchwork extending through Devil's Gulch into Helengon Gap. Large sections of the scenery between Sowbelly and French Gulch were also complete.

This brings us to John's philosophy of construction: "Rather than building all the mainline trackwork before scenicking, the two are often constructed together from a master plan of the railroad. Often the scenery is well along before ballast and ties are laid on the graded roadbed. Too much time spent consecutively on one type of construction bores me, and the variety and change in this method of hand-in-hand construction allows me any type of project at any time."

Scenery proceeded apace with tracklaying, and by December 1956 the dramatic bridges at French Gulch were in place and the scenery extended past them toward Drains. John continued westward during 1957 and early 1958, completing Drains and Robinson Cliff, extending the track around Sims Loop and into Squawbottom and Helengon Gap.

John recorded progress on the layout by taking panorama photos at regular intervals. The August 1958 panorama shows scenery complete as far as Squawbottom and Akin, and considerable progress at the Great Divide engine terminal. The turntable is installed, as are the service tracks radiating from it. The Cooper Electric trolley line trackwork is complete, but the trolley wire has not been installed.

Scenery techniques. —— Long before he started the new layout, John wrote: "Scenery is the one item in model railroading that you can't get in a kit. It's the big leveler between the man with lots of money and the fellow straining to make ends meet. The cost of the scenery will likely be the lightest part of a model railroad, yet the part most noticed...I don't just consider scenery as stuff to fill in between tracks to protect equipment from falling to the floor."

On the old layout, John had built terrain by first erecting a lattice of cardboard strips, then covering them with maga-zine paper dipped in starch. For the new G.D., with its scenery extending to the floor, he developed slightly different techniques. Scenery above the lowest track tier was formed with cardboard lattice strips as before, but John substituted brown wrapping paper and texture paint for the covering layer.

Scenery that extended from the lowest track to the floor had to be made of sterner stuff. Here, John substituted rough wood framing and large-mesh chicken wire for the lattice strips, draping the texture paint and brown paper covering over it. Where John had previously hand-carved rock faces, he now substituted cast plaster rock using rubber molds made from real rock. Much of the plaster used to make these rocks had some finely ground mica flakes added to it to give a granite-like crystalline sheen.

Real water on the layout was another scenic feature John had planned, one of the few that did not work out as expected. "Actual water will be used in the Port area, as well as in the log pond at Andrews. From Andrews the water will spill over numerous falls and rapids via Squawbottom Creek to a floor drain where Devil's Gulch joins Giant Canyon."

John waterproofed the harbor at Port, the log pond at Andrews, and the meandering route of Squawbotton Creek, but in 1968 he wrote to me: "I had planned originally to have the ferry floating on real water and I sealed the bottom of the harbor at Port for a depth of about 1½". However, after noting the humidity buildup in the railroad room from the real water in Andrews log pond and occasionally running Squawbottom Creek, I decided that the equivalent evaporating area of three or four bathtubs might be disadvantageous, so the 'water' at Port was simulated with a layer of clear casting plastic." By 1970 the water in the Andrews log pond was also replaced with such plastic.

Help with the work? —— One of the most-asked questions about the Gorre & Daphetid is how much work was done by others, especially servicemen from nearby bases who were on the operating crew. In asking this question of the people who were closest to the railroad I always got the same answer: "Very little."

Visitors often asked John if he'd built the whole railroad himself. Don Mitchell, one of the G.D. operators, relates: "I asked him that very question in 1962. John said that other people did less than 5 percent of the work...You couldn't touch an engine. You couldn't rerail a car—if your hands got near it you heard about it, too!"

When I interviewed the operators, no one was too sure just how much track had been laid by others. In the 1960s John's back began to trouble him badly, and both Jim Findley and Bill Corsa did some tracklaying. Darrell Harbin, one of the regular Tuesday night operators, often came on Thursday night to help with maintenance. Darrell told me: "I would do some wiring under the bench in places where it was difficult for John to reach. When the overhead on the trolley line was giving some trouble I crawled in there and resoldered some wire. Then I laid rail on the top level [the uppermost tier] behind Great Divide where John couldn't reach as well."

Several of the operators were quick to add that they didn't know whether John ripped out the track laid by others and relaid it afterward, or merely went over it to make a few adjustments. Jim Findley reported that the Cooper Electric trolley loop was principally the handiwork of Dave Cooper.

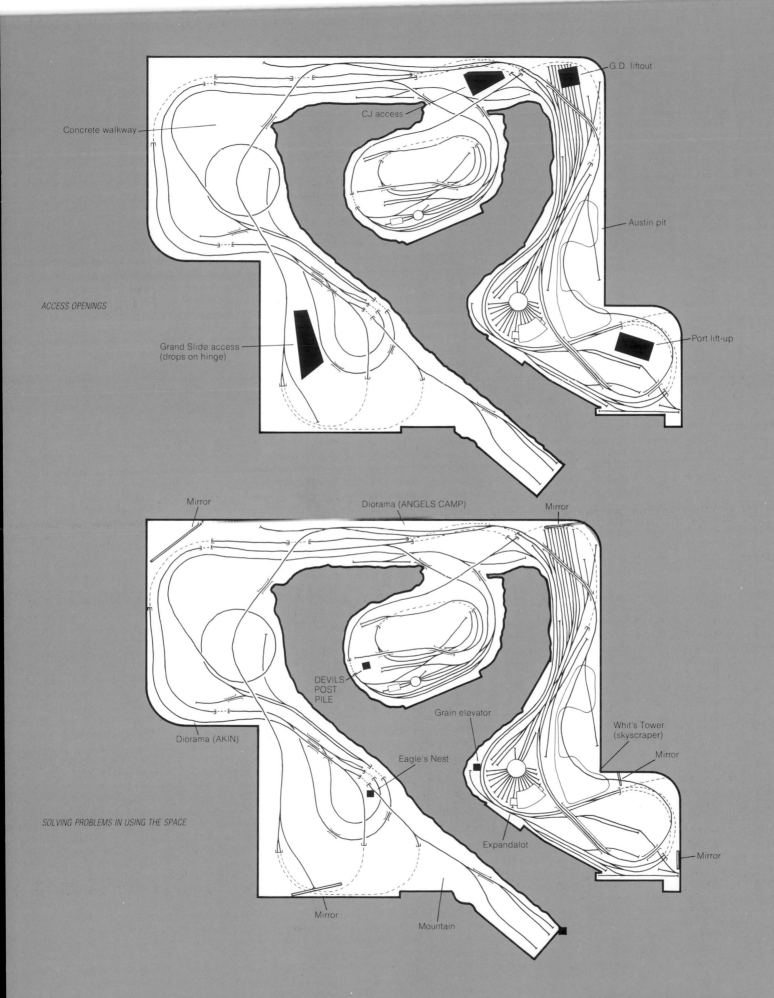

ACCESS OPENINGS

Concrete walkway

CJ access

G.D. liftout

Austin pit

Grand Slide access
(drops on hinge)

Port lift-up

Mirror

Diorama (ANGELS CAMP)

Mirror

SOLVING PROBLEMS IN USING THE SPACE

DEVILS
POST
PILE

Diorama (AKIN)

Grain elevator

Eagle's Nest

Whit's Tower
(skyscraper)

Mirror

Expandalot

Mirror

Mirror

Mountain

BUILDING THE EMPIRE **97**

The entire hillside area just to the left of Cross Junction was removable so that the three tiers of track behind it could be reached for repair or adjustment.

Dave made the poles and strung the wire, and John helped with the four-hand tasks. Beyond that, the only extensive help John accepted was from Jim Findley, in the form of the beautiful structures Jim scratchbuilt for the railroad.

A different kind of pace. —— By 1961, the nature of John's progress on the railroad had undergone a subtle change. The G.D. main line reached Eagle's Nest in 1961, but did not go beyond until 1967. The mountain area of the layout, which had progressed so quickly, was left incomplete while John worked on the cityscape at Port and Great Divide and various mechanical and electrical details. Also, the railroad was now being operated regularly, and this activity demanded more and more the of the time John had earlier devoted to construction.

The May 1961 panorama shows many of the structures in the cityscape either in place or roughed in, and the engine terminal at Great Divide fully detailed. In a letter to well-known model railroader Watson House, John wrote that structures slowed him down: "Buildings, with their ungodly number of windows, take lots of time and may get blocked out as to size and type years before final construction."

The year 1961 was especially productive for the G.D., but the years immediately following it were not. John had a heart attack during this period, and was also troubled by pains in his back and legs. In addition, like most of us, he occasionally lost interest in the hobby for two or three weeks, after which he would regain interest at full steam. In 1965, during a particularly low ebb, he wrote to the members of his operation round robin group: "This letter is later than its due

This four-photo panorama of the Gorre & Daphetid shows John's progress as of August 1, 1956, just three years after moving in. John's handwritten caption for this photo ended by saying: "I seem to have worked into a small club-type railroad without being one."

(Left) Eagle's Nest was a clever ruse to hide one of the support posts. The working lift cage, seen here halfway up the pinnacle, gave every HO scale passenger the ride of his life on the way to the top-of-the-mountain restaurant. (Above) Akin, the tiny settlement tucked in a corner behind Scalp Mountain, was modeled in forced perspective to make it appear a bit larger than it was. Most of the structures were smaller than HO scale.

(Above) By August 1958 John had completed 600 feet of track, 61 turnouts, and most of the scenery around Giant Canyon. Yet to come were the cityscape areas at Great Divide and Port, the wild region around Helengon Gap, Cold Shoulder, and the town of Andrews.

date, and I wish I could blame that upon the Christmas season rush, but that's not the reason. The fact is that I am at an all-time low towards interest in model railroading. This has been developing for more than a year, and I'm now at the point where I'm doubting if the hobby isn't too trite to pursue further. I've had periods in the past where I've left the hobby alone for a while and my enthusiasm gradually returned, but this time the interest seems to be getting less with time." The enthusiasm returned, however, and John wrote: "My interest in model railroading returned about three weeks after sending out my grumpy blast."

After his heart trouble, John lost about 50 pounds on his doctor's advice. He felt much better, and made substantial progress on the G.D. during 1965 and 1966. The panorama photos taken in January 1967 show the trackwork virtually complete at Port and at Great Divide save for the uppermost tier, many new structures in the cityscape, and the main line finally extended past Eagle's Nest toward Cold Shoulder, with a short branch into the new town of Andrews.

The moon over Great Divide. —— In the late '60s the nature of John's progress on the layout again changed subtly. Now the railroad was virtually complete, and he experimented with optical tricks, animation, and other refinements. In 1967 he added the hoist mechanism to animate the elevator to the restaurant at Eagle's Nest. In 1969 he wrote of his experiments with black lighting and fluorescent paints, and built the mechanism for the transition of the layout from day to night lighting. In this period he built the Expandalot parking lot under Great Divide terminal, and added the Compressed Space Company at Andrews, a tiny structure full of mirrors that appeared much larger inside than out.

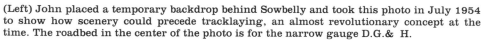

(Left) John placed a temporary backdrop behind Sowbelly and took this photo in July 1954 to show how scenery could precede tracklaying, an almost revolutionary concept at the time. The roadbed in the center of the photo is for the narrow gauge D.G.& H.

(Below) As the facade of the large Port station looms in the background, the bright yellow Cooper Electric trolley car trundles along Railroad Avenue toward it. The trolley line consisted of a simple loop of track, much of it hidden behind the buildings in Port and West Divide, and its operation was entirely automated.

The trickle of water down the rock face at the left of Helengon Gap is the source of Squawbottom Creek. John waterproofed the 45-foot-long concrete creek bed with the intention of having real running water in it most of the time. However, the water made the room very humid, so he decided against this feature.

Largely for reasons of accessibility, John built most of his scenery by starting at the rear edge of the layout and working forward. (Top right) Near Drains, he had almost completely detailed the terrain between the lowest track tier and the wall before starting on the scenery that extended to the floor. The bottom pair of photos shows how he applied paper and texture paint over large-mesh chicken wire. After this dried he added plaster rock castings.

One of the operators, Perry Jenkins, told me how John showed off these little changes: "He was always doing things to the layout and not telling us, wondering how long it would take us to notice them. It was not until the third operating session that anyone noticed the working chase lights on the little theater marquee [in Austin]."

In August 1970 John designed one of his most captivating special effects, the moon over Great Divide. This ruse consisted of a 2″ diameter cardboard disk and a piece of music wire attached to a clock motor which turned at six revolu-

(Above) This was the Gorre & Daphetid in April 1961. The engine terminal is in use, and Port and Great Divide are just beginning to take shape. John has just completed the impressive Squaw Creek High Bridge and the double-track truss over the harbor at Port.

tions per hour. The mechanism was mounted behind the mirror at Great Divide passenger station, and after the railroad room changed over to night lighting, the moon would slowly swing up from behind the mirror, move in a 22″ diameter arc, and disappear behind the mirror again before daylight returned. The moon, colored with fluorescent paint, glowed pale yellow and was visible for about 5 minutes.

John's last panorama, taken in August 1971, shows major progress in several areas. The main line reached Cold Shoulder in July 1971, and scenery in the Helengon Gap alcove was finished soon after. Port and Great Divide were complete and almost fully detailed, including final touches on the background. All track, save for the two great bridges across Giant Canyon, the uppermost tier viaduct over Great Divide passenger yard, and the narrow gauge, was in place.

The Gorre & Daphetid that we visited in the first two chapters of this book is the layout as it existed late in 1972. John's very late photos show that the great steel arch bridge between Cold Shoulder and Scalp Mountain was completed in January 1972, and one of the last touches he added before his death in 1973 was the tiny live steam club railroad under the viaduct at Gorre.

John never said much about future projects for the railroad, preferring to spring surprises on his operators. His sketchbooks, however, reveal plans for several features he planned to add. First, of course, was the Devil's Gulch Bridge, the last of the G.D.'s spectacular spans. John's drawings show two designs, one a half through arch, the other a towering suspension bridge. Another new feature was to be a cable car system. This was to start under the masonry arch near Cross Junction station, proceed up the steep street behind the station, disappear behind the building with the clock at Great Divide, and terminate behind the mirror. The track was to have a slot between the rails, and the cars were to be powered by an endless belt.

Throughout the last years of the G.D. the layout was operated by the regular crew almost every Tuesday night. One thing I haven't described yet is how John wired the railroad for realistic operation. We'll take up that subject next.

Expandalot, built in 1968, made use of mirrors to generate the impression of a cavernous underground parking lot beneath Great Divide engine terminal. Actually, there were only two model cars inside, each painted different colors front and rear.

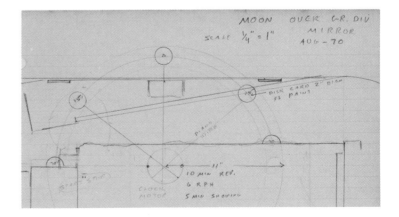

This is John's August 1970 sketch for the "Moon over Great Divide," one of the most striking of his night lighting effects.

(Above) These photos were taken in January 1967. The top view shows the branch to Andrews completed, and Cold Shoulder gradually taking shape. The center and bottom photos reveal considerable progress on the cityscape at Great Divide and Port.

(Right) Jim Findley scratchbuilt several exquisite structures for the G.D., including this delicate see-through gasholder at Port.

(Below) The July 1971 panorama shows the G.D. nearly complete. Still missing are the two great bridges on either side of Scalp Mountain, the upper tier track over Great Divide yard, the narrow gauge loop at Helengon, and the lift bridge across the harbor at Port.

This unusual 1972 view from Sowbelly shows the huge Scalp Mountain Arch Bridge, the last bridge John built. The little settlement on the left side of the photo is Daphetid.

"This is the golden age of a model railroad. The builder always has plenty of new projects to construct, yet because there is enough done for good operation, the need for more to be done is not urgent if you don't feel like doing it."

Operating the G.D. Line

OPERATION was just as important to John Allen as the appearance of his railroad. The Gorre & Daphetid came alive during operation, and not just because the train movements added action and animation to its scenes. John enjoyed sharing model railroading with others, and every G.D. operating session got several people involved in the challenging and entertaining task of making the layout perform as a functional railroad. Because operation is a difficult topic to explain with words and pictures in limited space, this aspect of the Gorre & Daphetid received little coverage in magazines.

To properly understand the how and why of the G.D. operating scheme, we should first look at how John set up the controls. The layout was wired using the "independent rail" method, meaning that each control block was electrically independent from every other (in contrast to "common rail," where most blocks use a common electrical return path). The

French Gulch is once again the scene for dramatic action as a westbound ore train on the wood Howe deck truss rolls downgrade toward Squawbottom while a local mail train from Andrews speeds toward Port on the tier above.

main line was divided into 17 blocks, each of which could be assigned to any one of the three mainline cabs.

The large control panel at Gorre was divided into four sections. On the left end were Cab 1 and a blank space reserved for the controls of the narrow gauge D.G.& H. In the center was a large mimic diagram of the layout which John called the "CTC Board." This diagram had turnout controls and center-off switches that assigned mainline blocks either to Cab 1, by throwing the toggle to the left, or to Cab 2, by throwing the toggle to the right. Cab 2 was to the right of the CTC board, and on the right end of the panel was Cab 3, which included a row of rectangular pushbuttons similar to those on automobile radios. Each button connected two mainline blocks to Cab 3. Cab 3 could select blocks only when the toggle on the CTC board was in the "off" position, that is, when the blocks were not in use by Cab 1 or Cab 2.

Local panels at Great Divide, Port, and Andrews controlled the yard tracks, but allowed trains to enter and depart under the control of a mainline cab. John wrote: "When their trains are within yard limits at Port and Great Divide, mainline engineers operate according to tower signals that are set by the yard operators. The mainline engineers retain control of their trains' movements, but obey the yard operators' signal indications...Turnouts in the yards are controlled by the yard operators. Out on the line, train crews throw the turnouts. Mainline engineers use whistle signals to announce their approach to track [not highway] crossings at

grade and to call the yard operators' attention when reaching yard limits."

Six blocks had signals at trackside, and three of those indications were repeated on control panels. Two of the signals showed turnout position. Most turnouts on the main line were operated remotely by rotary-relay switch machines, and their toggle handles on the main panel indicated the turnout position. Other buttons and switches operated solenoid uncoupling ramps, signal whistles, and the fast clock.

The water meter and the flywheel throttle. —— Cab 1, Cab 2, and the throttles for the yard panels had conventional rheostat speed controls, but Cabs 2 and 3 incorporated some special wrinkles. On Cab 2, John rigged up a device to simulate the water in a steam locomotive tender: "For a number of years I have been endeavoring to make the running of a loco have more of the prototype problems and controls. The engineer job on most model railroads is too easy, except where the engineer is also serving as his own conductor on a switching run. One of my gadgets is the 'water meter.' Actually, it is a fuel meter, as it registers the amount of electricity used by the locomotive.

"I use an old house meter in which the magnets are broken, so it runs much faster than it should. Hooked up in the 115-volt line to the cab [Cab 2] power supply, the meter revolves in proportion to the power consumed, actuating a delicate contact once each revolution. This in turn operates a

(Above) The whirring driveshaft and thrashing siderods of Heisler-geared locomotive number 6 belie her rather leisurely speed of only 12 scale miles per hour. Maintaining prototypical scale speeds was no problem at all for the G.D.'s naturally slow geared logging engines.

(Left) The G.D.'s "Pacific Scale Time" clock was located in a tall building at Great Divide so it could be seen from all panels and operating positions. This pre-1967 photo shows Cross Junction before Jim Findley built his handsome two-level station for the site.

(Opposite page) Here, on the big mainline control panel at Gorre, Cabs 1 and 2 flank what John termed the "CTC Board," which housed the controls that connected mainline blocks to the cabs. Cab 3, the flywheel throttle, is out of sight to the right of this photo.

pinball machine counter at the engineer's controls. Since water consumption, not fuel, is the usual range limitation for a steam locomotive, I call the counter a water indicator. I decide how far each engine should be able to go on one filling and then rate its tender accordingly.

"I decided the largest tender holds 1000 counter units, and that the others hold proportionately less, down to only 200 units for the Shay. Most tenders are rated at 500 to 600 units. When operating, you cannot run without water units. Out on the line, you must stop, no matter where, if you use up the water. Then, another engine and a tank car will have to bring enough to get you to the next tank. Obviously, an engineer won't pass a water plug without refilling unless he is sure he can reach the next one. You learn by experience, and believe me, you appreciate a large tender when your engine has one."

The flywheel throttle in Cab 3 was John's real gem. "If you're going to run a train, you should run it like a train. But with a plain rheostat, or even a variable transformer for a throttle, you hardly feel like an engineer. An engineer on the real thing has problems to solve. He's got to build up speed as he approaches a grade so the train's momentum will carry it up as far as possible. At the same time, an engine can go only so fast, or there may be a speed restriction for the territory. A good engineer, with a steady hand on the throttle, with knowledge of the grades, the wind, and the day's weather, and taking into account the length and weight of his train, could run a steam engine up to 20 percent farther on his load of water...That's why I built my flywheel throttle the way I did."

John described this ingenious throttle in the *NMRA Bulletin*. He used two war-surplus 28-volt DC motors, wiring one of them as a DC generator. He connected the motors with a common shaft on which he mounted a 4″ diameter, 1″ thick metal flywheel, building, in effect, a miniature motor-generator set. By regulating the speed of the motor from the control panel and feeding the output of the generator to the track, John achieved realistic momentum and horsepower effects, effects that challenged the mainline engineer using Cab 3.

Time, speed, and "smiles." —— G.D. trains operated according to written time schedules and the fast clock located in one of the buildings near the passenger terminal at Great Divide. About 1950 John had altered this clock with friction gearing so he could experiment with different time ratios. He found that he liked a 12:1 ratio best, where five minutes of real time equaled one hour of scale time. The on-off switch for the clock was on the panel at Gorre.

John wrote extensively on the subject of scale time: "Surprisingly, some operating model rails don't understand the reasons or advantages of scale time, and even doubt if the principle of scaling down time is logical. Some think scale time is only for the purpose of making a time schedule more

OFFICIAL DISTANCES ON THE G.D. LINE		
Actual feet	**Location**	**Smilepost**
0	Great Divide (station crossover)	0
18	Cross Junction (via cutoff)	4.4
36	Gorre (station)	7.2
42	Gorre (east switch)	8
49	Sowbelly (team track switch)	10.4
87	Squawbottom (west switch)	17.4
97	Squawbottom (east switch)	19
151	Cross Junction	31
163	Port (yard limit)	32.6
191	Port (east crossover)	38
214	Corsa (switch)	44
249	Akin (station)	50.6
262	Eagle's Nest (west switch)	52.4
268	Andrews (switch)	53.6
284	Cold Shoulder (switch)	56.8
296	Scalp	59.2
316	Angels Camp (west switch)	62.8
327	West Divide (switch)	65.4
370	Great Divide (end of track)	74
	Measurements are to switch points	
	One smile = 5 feet	

John wrote up this table of distances in April 1964. In one or two cases the distance in smiles does not exactly equal the distance in feet divided by five, which indicates that John considered factors other than distance alone in making up his operating schedules.

Cab three's flywheel momentum throttle was built from two 28-volt DC motors, a hefty metal flywheel, some scraps of wood, and plenty of electrical tape. It may not have been much to look at, but operating a mainline train with it was a real challenge for the engineer.

impressive, and has no practical operating advantages...It has even been suggested that the term 'scale time' is inexact, and the proper term should be 'fast time.' These people claim that time is a absolute and cannot logically be scaled.

"Nonsense! The term 'scale time' is absolutely correct; that's exactly what it is, scaled down time. There is no difference between scaling time and scaling dimensions, they are both fantasy for the sake of realism." John went on to explain that the ratio of scale time to real time depended on the distances on your railroad and the type of operation you wish to conduct. "Generally, the longer the distance between stations, the longer the scale minute can become...and the faster the train speeds, the more necessary it is to have shorter scale minutes."

Of timetables, John wrote to Cliff Robinson: "A timetable sets up the order of operation, the meeting places, and the times of arrival and departure from yards. It also requires a set of rules of precedence. For example, a yard crew should know when a train must be made up to leave, when other trains are due in, and thus, how much time it has to classify cars or switch local industries. If the crew can't get all the work done in the time allowed, it should know which work has lower priority and so can be left for the next run. By looking ahead at the schedule of arrivals and departures the yard crew can better allocate its time between switching industries and classifying cars...I prefer to work by time...The timetable system takes a load off the dispatcher and requires more decisions by the train crews."

"Working against a clock—that is, getting your work done on time without speeding loco movements or otherwise breaking prototype rules—can provide a feeling of purpose and accomplishment as well as develop your operating skills. You will hold up many scheduled arrivals and departures while you learn, but gradually you will develop the exper-

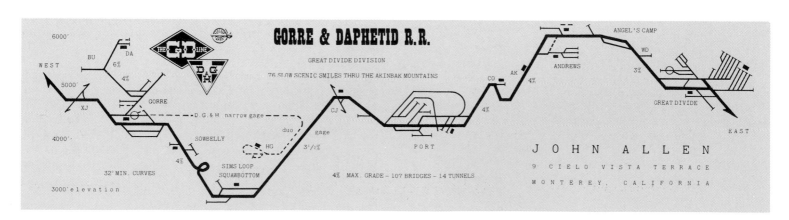

John devised this letterhead to use when writing letters to other model railroaders who were interested in realistic operation. The schematic diagram is unusual in that it includes elevations as well as track arrangements along the line.

ience and skill to be classified as a real operating man."

John was an early proponent of running trains at realistic scale speeds. "Just as you can tell a fine modelbuilder by the way he lifts and handles a model, you can tell a fine operator by the way he handles a train and by the speed he runs it. It is almost a rule of thumb that the finer and more appreciative the operator, the closer to scale speeds he runs.

"Slow speed helps to make the time a train is out on the line comparable to its switching time, and has the effect of increasing the length of the railroad. On the G.D. we have slowly and continually reduced our average speed for all trains. Besides making the trains look better on our tight interurban-like curves, this gives us greater separation between stations. Realistic acceleration and deceleration rates are carefully maintained, with or without inertia-type throttles. Average freight speeds have dropped from 30 miles per hour down to 20, and average passenger speeds from 45 down to 30 or 35. Believe it or not, we have come to the point where we feel we are really rolling at speeds of 35 miles per hour and up."

John devised a gadget to encourage smooth train handling and switching. He mounted a trough-like pair of rails inside a boxcar body, and placed a large ball bearing on it, allowing the ball to roll freely. When the car was subjected to rough handling, the ball rolled off the end of the rails, lighting a bright red bulb under the car. He wrote: "The crews of the G.D. Line have usually been rather careful about train handling, but with the new device we found we took more care than ever. It improved our operating skill. Just for fun we sometimes grouse about the sneaky management while we are switching with the impact car in our train, just as the prototype crews do [John was referring here to the impact recorders used by real railroads to register shocks and assign responsibility for in-transit damage], but actually we all enjoy working with the indicator cars."

G.D. distances were expressed in "smiles." John wrote: "When a modeler uses a scale time ratio, he should use the same ratio to further reduce his scale mile, which is called—to borrow a term from the late Frank Ellison—a 'smile.' If you operate in HO, your scale mile is 60.6 feet—let's call it 60 feet for simplicity. If you use 6:1 scale time, your mile is also reduced 6:1 and your mile becomes 10 feet. To differentiate it from the scale mile, it is called a 'smile.' This keeps everything in relation: a model locomotive traveling 60 scale miles per hour will take the same time (1 minute) to travel a scale mile as its prototype takes for a full mile, and its drivers will revolve at the same rate. With scale time and smiles, this loco, traveling with the exact same driver revolution speed, will still go 1 smile in 1 minute, whether the ratio is 6:1 or any other ratio.

"The principal stumbling block in the acceptance of scale time has been confusion over the use of the scaled-down mile. At a 10:1 ratio, for instance, a smile is 6 feet in HO or 11 feet in O scale. This is no longer than a locomotive and 10 cars, but you cannot accept the fact that a train is a mile long. It becomes simpler if you realize that it isn't necessary to think of smiles except for scheduling. I do mark out distances along my railroad in smiles from a zero point—bridges and stations are numbered according to the 'smiles' from zero—but I seldom think of smiles except in time schedule operation. For me, scale time and smiles are strictly for schedule operation and don't apply visually or in construction."

Because John used 12:1 scale time, a G.D. smile was 5 feet. In a chart that John drew up in 1964, he calculated that the completed main line (Great Divide to Cross Junction, through Gorre, and back to Great Divide) would be 370 actual feet long, or 74 smiles, a reasonable length for a prototype mountain division.

The operating crew. —— It took a crew of five to ten men to operate the G.D. as John had designed it, and until the late 1960s, when John finally managed to find a group of local model railroaders who showed up on time for the weekly operating sessions, many of the operators were servicemen from the nearby military bases. In 1964 he wrote: "Our crews are a constant change. Seldom does one operator stay here in Monterey more than three years; most are here only six months to a year before their job moves them. I'm sure there are at least 100 model railroaders who have operated more or less regularly here for from six weeks to three years. Most had no previous operating experience, and many were introduced to the hobby here."

Andy Sperandeo, who was in the Army and stationed at Fort Ord, tells of the crews in 1970 and 1971: "The regular group included several fellows from the Monterey area: Joe Cain, Allan Fenton, Earl Flaws, and Darrel Harbin. Bill Corsa had been a regular before moving to Walnut Grove, and he occasionally managed to make the long drive down to Monterey. Russ Cain, no relation to Joe, also became a regular before I left. One other operator who has to be mentioned was John's good friend Jim Findley. Jim was still working in Korea at the time, but he was able to visit frequently.

"The group was primarily for operating the railroad, although the Monterey guys did go as a group to the quarterly Coast Division NMRA meetings and Pacific Coast Region NMRA conventions. John was not a part of this activity in the fall, however. The Coast Division meets were held on Sundays, and John was an avid pro football fan. Came autumn and John gave precedence to the NFL over the NMRA."

The Gorre & Daphetid's impact cars registered rough handling during train handling and switching. When the large ball bearing inside rolled off its track into either end pocket, it completed an electrical circuit and lit a red bulb beneath the car.

EASTBOUND

	Passenger 4	Freight 12	Fast Gas-Electric 8	Long Through Freight 14	Freight 16	Passenger 6	Freight 10
Great Divide							
Leave	8:05 AM	11:05 AM	2:01 PM	2:40 PM	6:05	9:01	1:50
Cross Junction	8:20 AM	11:20 AM	2:15 PM (Siding)	3:01 PM	6:20 (Siding)	9:15 (Siding)	2:01
Gorre							
Arrive	8:30 AM	11:30 AM	2:30 PM		6:30	9:30	
Leave	8:35 AM	11:35 AM	5:20 PM	3:20	8:01	11:01	2:10
Sowbelly					8:20		
Squawbottom							
Arrive	9:20 AM	12:15 PM	6:00 PM		8:55	12:01	2:45
Leave	9:30 AM	12:30 PM	6:50 PM	4:01	9:40	12:30	3:01
Cross Junction	10:20 AM	1:15 PM	7:40	4:50	10:30	1:20	
Port							
Arrive	10:50 AM	1:40 PM	7:55	5:15 PM	10:50	1:45	4:00

WESTBOUND

	Freight 11	Passenger 5	Slow Freight 13	Freight 15	Gas-Electric 9	Freight 17	Passenger 7
Port							
Leave	8:05 AM	11:30	2:15	5:40	8:15	11:15	2:01
Cross Junction	8:30	11:50	2:40	6:01	8:40	11:35	2:20
Squawbottom							
Arrive	9:15		3:30				
Leave	9:30	12:30 PM	4:05	6:45	9:30	12:20	2:55
Sowbelly							
Gorre							
Arrive						1:05	
Leave	10:30	1:15	5:01	7:30	10:25	1:10	3:40
Cross Junction	10:45	1:30	5:15	7:45	10:40	1:25	3:50
Great Divide							
Arrive	11:00 AM	1:45	5:30	8:00	10:55	1:40	4:01

There were several G.D. operating schedules, and John refined each of them over the years. This schedule from his planning notebook was labeled "number 2," and shows the point-to-loop-and-back scheme used to operate the railroad in the late 1960s.

John said of the crews in 1961: "I'll welcome new operators whether or not they contribute much during the bull session, though of course it is most pleasant when they do. Unlike Whit [Towers] and Cliff [Robinson], most of my operating group are not close personal friends. Most of us only see each other during an operating session...Other than the operation itself, the session is run very informally. There are no dues, no officers, nor obligation to work on the railroad. Participation is by my invitation, but that is most easy to acquire by showing an interest to operate."

John assigned either one- or two-man train crews. In 1961 he wrote of using two men per train: "I find the conductor and engineer on my system have about an equal amount of work to do. The conductor does more thinking, but if he's inexperienced, the engineer will help. The engineer job requires more knowledge of the board [control panel] and skill with train control, particularly with the flywheel acceleration throttle...Many operators don't care to be paired because it can spoil some of the fun for them. For example, an engineer may think he knows a better way to make a certain switching move than his conductor is willing to try. The conductor is boss of the train, so the idea may never be tested."

Tuesday nights at John's. —— Tuesday was the regular

G.D. operating night while Andy Sperandeo was in the operating group, and almost every week the crew gathered in John's living room between 7:30 and 8:00. Andy described the start of a session: "When everyone arrived John led us down to the basement. The business of getting organized and assigning jobs didn't take long, and was usually based on our individual preferences and John's appreciation of each man's abilities. There were eight regular operating positions at that time: Great Divide yardmaster, Great Divide roundhouse foreman, a mainline engineer to run through freights and passenger trains, a Gorre-to-Daphetid branchline engineer, a Gorre peddler engineer for the Gorre-Port way freight, a Port yardmaster/West Port yard engineer, an East Port yard engineer, and an Andrews engineer to run the Andrews-Port peddler and the interchange trains."

If there were less than eight people some of these jobs were eliminated. First to go would be the Great Divide roundhouse foreman, followed by the East Port engineer and the Andrews engineer. With six or seven operators the group could still run all the trains, but with only five John dropped freights between Port and Andrews from the schedule. Andy continues: "With less than five we couldn't run the schedule John was then using, and we usually stayed upstairs for talk and the Timesaver switching game. We didn't often have

(Above) The passing siding at Squawbottom had two industries located on it, which meant that trains that took the siding, such as the Gorre peddler, had to move and reposition cars spotted there. This Shay-powered log train is about to tackle the stiff grade up to Sowbelly.

(Right) Train number 8, the local passenger run from Great Divide to Port and Andrews, rounds Sims Loop headed downgrade to Squawbottom. This train is usually handled by gas-electric car 60, but this morning the train rates Ten-Wheeler No. 49 and a three-car heavyweight consist.

more than eight, but if we did, two people would pair up so that one of them could learn a new job from the other."

In later years John seemed to like the Gorre branchline job best, although he would take a turn at the other positions from time to time. Darrel Harbin regularly handled the Gorre peddler, Earl Flaws liked either the through-train runs or the Andrews job, and Joe Cain would most often take either the Great Divide roundhouse or Andrews. Allan Fenton was almost as proficient as John at handling any job on the railroad.

After cleaning the track wiper cars, the first step was to determine where in the schedule the last session had ended, so the operators would know what to do to pick up the action. John didn't necessarily run only one 24-hour cycle each week. Some sessions might be as short as 18 to 20 scale hours, others would run as long as 30 scale hours. When John decided the crews had been at it long enough the session simply stopped, and the operators pulled switch cuts and trains into sidings so John would have the main line clear for entertaining visitors.

Two through freights ran in each direction between

Great Divide and Port: an afternoon fast freight limited to the number of boxcars that a single engine could handle (reefers and stock cars could be included to fill out tonnage), and an early morning slow freight that took anything except boxcars up to a length of 26 cars (the safe limit rounding Sims Loop), double-headed if necessary by the G.D.'s heaviest engines. By seeing whether the yards had cars for the fast freight or the slow freight the operators knew where to pick up the schedule.

Scheduled trains. —— Because the main line hadn't been finished through Cold Shoulder or across Devil's Gulch, the schedules in use in the early '70s treated the Great Divide-Gorre-Port section as an out-and-back main using the reverse loop at Port. The section from Port to Andrews operated as a branch, as did the Gorre-Daphetid portion of the line. The stub to Cold Shoulder was used as an interchange connection with Jim Findley's Tioga Pass RR. No trains served Angels Camp.

The schedule included the following trains:
●Slow freights 14 and 15 from Great Divide to Port and

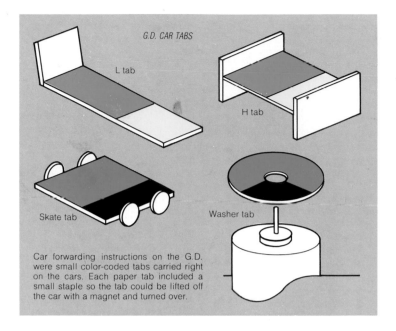

G.D. CAR TABS

L tab

H tab

Skate tab

Washer tab

Car forwarding instructions on the G.D. were small color-coded tabs carried right on the cars. Each paper tab included a small staple so the tab could be lifted off the car with a magnet and turned over.

•Fast freights 34 and 35, the afternoon freight run from Great Divide to Port and back. A 2-8-2, either No. 40 or No. 42, or the 2-8-4, No. 45, was the usual fast freight power.

•Mail trains 6 and 7, a nighttime local from Great Divide through Port to Andrews and return. Train 7 backed down the grade from Andrews because there was no way to turn its engine there, but after it backed into the Port passenger station it could run forward to Great Divide. Train 7 picked up the red combine that had been left at Gorre by No. 8 and returned it to Great Divide.

In addition to the combine on trains 8 and 7, freights 14, 15, 34, and 35 operated as mixed trains between Great Divide and Gorre to provide local passenger service between those points and Daphetid. The G.D.'s long caboose-combine or drovers' caboose was coupled behind the regular caboose out of Great Divide on trains 14 and 34. At Gorre this car was set out and the branchline engineer had to take it to Daphetid and back to Gorre in time to connect with train 15 or 35 back to Great Divide.

These five round trips out of Great Divide, ten scheduled trains in all, were usually handled by the mainline engineer, who operated from Cab 3 on the Gorre control board. The other scheduled trains were run by the Andrews operator. These were the Tioga Pass interchange trains, 41, 42, 43, and 44. The mainline stub to Cold Shoulder was used as a staging track for these trains, and 41 was scheduled to leave there and arrive at Port about an hour after 15 had left. Train 41 would leave its cars at Port, pick up any cars bound for the interchange, and return as No. 42. Trains 43 and 44 were similarly scheduled to work in and out of Port an hour after No. 35's departure. These trains were often powered by Tioga Pass locomotives to represent the connecting line.

back. Number 14 set out eastbound shortly after midnight, and westbound 15 did not tie up until after dawn. If more cars would be on 14 out of Gorre or 15 out of Port than one engine could handle on the grades, 14 would leave Great Divide double-headed. These were the runs where 4-10-0 No. 34 and the various articulateds earned their keep.

•Gas-electric locals 8 and 9, from Great Divide through Port to Andrews, and return. These morning schedules were protected by car No. 60, which the G.D. operators called the "gasatronic." Number 8 pulled a short red combine from Great Divide to Gorre, where it was left for the branchline engineer to deliver to Daphetid.

•Fast passenger trains 4 and 5, a noontime turnaround trip from Great Divide to Port and back, with stops only at Gorre and Squawbottom. The equipment on these trains was either 4-6-2 No. 56 with John's red streamlined consist, or engine 50 with Pullman green heavyweights.

Peddler runs. —— The peddler freights to and from Gorre and Andrews worked as informal extras—informal because there was no dispatcher to issue running orders for them— and they made as many round trips as they could while staying clear of the scheduled trains. The Gorre peddler worked between Gorre and Port, switching Sowbelly, Squawbottom, and Cross Junction. From the track plan it may not seem that

Struggling upgrade across Squaw Creek High Bridge, the Andrews peddler approaches Eagle's Nest. Andrews itself is just beyond, at far left. While both locomotives are typical of the older G.D. power used on the Andrews peddler, it was unusual for this train to rate a helper engine. It usually doubled the hill from Port instead.

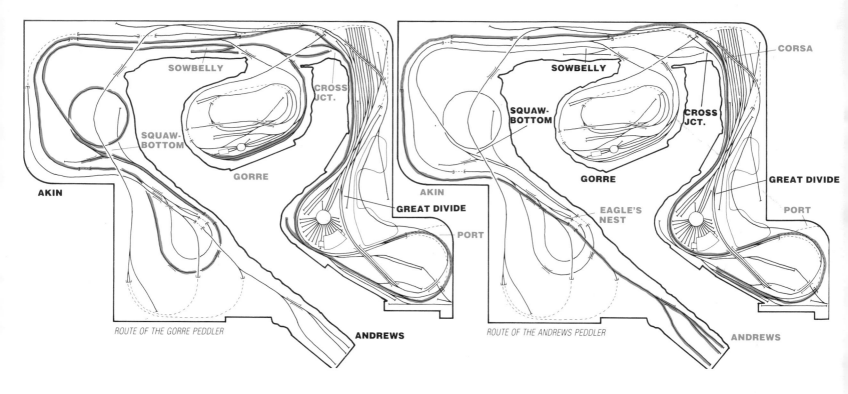

there was a lot for this train to do, but there were a couple of industries located along the Squawbottom passing siding. Not only did these add switching spots, they further complicated life for the Gorre peddler by requiring that it move and respot cars whenever it had to meet a through train at Squawbottom. Just to make things a little tougher, whenever the peddler had more cars for some other industry than the spur could accommodate, the only place it could store them was on the Squawbottom siding.

Squawbottom wasn't the only place where the Gorre peddler had to make tricky meets. Occasionally the peddler had to meet a through train between Squawbottom and Port, a long stretch without a passing siding. It did this by heading or backing onto the Cross Junction interchange track, blocking the Great Divide to Gorre main line while the through run came by Cross Junction. This let the peddler get over the road faster than if it had waited at Squawbottom, and helped avoid even more complicated meets at Port.

The Gorre peddler could be a short train or a long one, and it sometimes left Port with more than 20 cars. Even worse, it sometimes brought that many into the congested yard at Port. Its usual engine was either 2-6-6-2 No. 38 or a similar Sierra RR. model owned by Bill Corsa when he ran the train. When Darrel Harbin ran the Gorre peddler, as he often did, he used the only diesel locomotive ever allowed to operate regularly on the G.D. He had reworked and detailed a Trains Incorporated EMD TR4 cow-and-calf set. They were smooth-running, powerful, and good looking, and John was sufficiently impressed to let Darrel use them on the Gorre peddler.

The Andrews peddler ran between Andrews and Port. Its main business was switching Andrews, but it also worked the coal trestle spur at Corsa (the upper level of the bi-level Cross Junction station). The Andrews engineer had to time these runs so as not to conflict with the interchange trains or the other scheduled runs on the branch. It also helped if he

coordinated closely with the Port yardmaster, although the peddler was usually quite welcome in Port because cars bound for Andrews often backed up there.

The Andrews peddler run was home for several older, smaller engines. Sometimes it would have a 2-8-0 like No. 26 or No. 28, which could each take ten cars up the hill, or perhaps a Tioga Pass 2-8-0 or 2-10-0. It might also have 0-6-0 No. 12 or 2-6-0 No. 25, which could only take six cars. Often Port would have more cars for Andrews than these engines could handle, so the extra cars would have to wait for the next trip.

Occasionally the Andrews engineer would have time to double the hill and so could take more cars than the peddler engine's rating. The procedure in these cases was to have the peddler start through the Railroad Avenue crossover and pull as far as it could up the Andrews line with the full train. As the grade started right past the crossover the peddler wouldn't get very far before it stalled. The West Port switcher would then run around the balloon track and shove the peddler clear of the crossover. With the rear of his train out of the way at Port, the Andrews engineer could head up the hill with the front half of his train, returning later for the rest. The Port yardmaster was always glad to help the peddler get as many cars as possible out of Port.

Yard jobs, and the bottleneck at Port. —— The Great Divide yardmaster was responsible for dispatching and receiving the scheduled mainline trains, and also for assigning motive power and servicing the industries at Great Divide. His task was complicated by having his classification yard face backwards to the main line as it then was. This meant that once he had a train ready to go, he would have to pull it, tail first, onto the high bridge over Port with his switcher and let it sit there while he coupled the road locomotive onto the head end. The Great Divide yard was then effectively tied up until the train left. When a roundhouse foreman was

Eastbound passenger trains arriving at Port ran around the loop and arrived at the terminal headed back toward Great Divide. This passenger consist is on its way to the station.

available to hostle engines and switch some of the industries it considerably eased the yardmaster's load.

The Gorre branchline engineer's job included preparing blocks of cars for the through freights and the Gorre peddler, switching the industries at Gorre, serving the Daphetid branch including the Butler mine on the switchback, and making the passenger runs with the combines from Great Divide. This was John's favorite job, and though he knew it better than anyone else he generally had to keep his Shay moving continuously to get everything done on schedule.

John built this light-duty marine railway for the Port boatyard early in 1972. He planned to replace the temporary girder bridge at right with a lifting type to allow ships access to the basin.

Every train on the railroad except the branchline runs to Daphetid passed through Port. There were also more than a dozen industries to serve at Port, as well as the car ferry *Anabel* which could only be worked twice a day between the hours of 12 and 5 (at other times it was presumed underway). The yard facilities were inadequate, in part deliberately to add to the challenge, but also because there was no room at Port to build more tracks. It was a hot spot, even with two engineers.

With two engineers the West Port man would switch the grain elevator siding, the ferry, and the industries along the two long spurs beyond the ferry slip. West Port also classified cars for the Andrews and Gorre peddlers, stashing these cars on one of the long tracks on the front side of the basin. The East Port engineer's main job was to classify cars for the through freights, using one of the long straight tracks as the make-up track and sorting from the other. The East Port switcher also worked the industries on the switchback at the freight station, and the spurs on the front side of the basin. By cooperatively shoving cars past each other's engines the two Port engineers could avoid runaround movements. The two also cooperated in spotting cars for the interchange trains west of the Railroad Avenue crossover.

Andy Sperandeo remembers Port: "When I first began to operate at East Port, John had just installed that board on a suggestion from Cliff Robinson, and he was trying to use one of the Little Joe ["Dockside"] 0-4-0Ts as the East Port switch engine. The long cuts that had to be handled when classifying the through freights were too much for so small a locomotive, and when John ran East Port he got into the habit of pushing the engine with his finger when he had too many cars on it. Seeing him do it I began doing the same thing myself, as did a couple of the others.

"One night before we went downstairs John announced that he had noticed this most unprototypical practice, and admitted having some part in it himself, but that from then on overloaded locomotives would not be helped by giant hands from the sky. One of the first things I noticed when we went downstairs was that the 0-4-0T at East Port had been replaced by one of the G.D.'s sturdy Shays.

"That wasn't quite the end of shenanigans with the East

The Port operator (in later years there were two) had only this tiny three-track yard in which to sort cars arriving from all over the Gorre & Daphetid. To add to his problems, the car ferry had to be switched twice in every 24-hour operating period.

Port switch engine. If the Shay was facing east, with all its cylinders and drive motion toward the operators and viewers, the gear covers on its trucks would foul the decking of the pier which supported the switchback. Putting operating efficiency ahead of aesthetic concerns, I'd run the Shay around the balloon track before starting to work at East Port. The interesting mechanical stuff might be out of sight, but the old girl could get where she had to go without tripping. Apparently John keenly felt the loss of all that nice sidewinder action, for on the following week I'd return to find the Shay facing east again."

The tab-on-car system. —— Freight car routing on the G.D. was by a system of four-step, color-coded tabs carried on top of the cars. Each tab had a sequence of routing information to send its car through a series of four different destinations. The tabs were made of stiff paper or card, but they had bits of staple or pinheads in them that allowed them to be lifted from the cars with magnets. (John said he didn't care how dusty the roofs of his cars became as long as nobody left fingerprints in the dust.)

John had tried card-order and switchlist routing in the early '60s, but they hadn't been what he was looking for. He wanted a system oriented toward the train and switch crews, one that produced problems appropriate to crew rather than management solutions. In 1962 he wrote to Watty House: "The emphasis on my railroad is on the train crew, not the car distributor. The train crew cares little what is in the car; their only problem is to deliver it to an interchange point or final destination." John also didn't care whether a car was theoretically loaded or empty, but only if a model locomotive could actually pull it up a hill.

John sought a random distribution of traffic that would produce a realistic ebb and flow of car movements, rather than a cut-and-dried, programmed number of cars assigned to each train. He especially did not want operators making decisions about what cars to send where during a session, which he felt was like letting players make up the rules of a game as they went along.

The tab-on-car system, which John started using in 1964, did what he wanted it to, but he recognized its disadvantages. The tabs didn't look prototypical, and he had to remove most of them from the cars for photography. (Of course, one of the system's advantages was that the tabs could be removed without leaving a trace, since the cars weren't modified.) He also would have liked to retain the car identification feature of card and list systems, so an operator could think of moving SFRD reefer 24389 rather than a "blue C." On balance, however, he felt the tab system was the best way to get the kind of action he wanted.

Each destination or group of destinations was assigned a color. Great Divide was white, Gorre and the Daphetid branch were yellow, Gorre peddler destinations—Sowbelly, Squawbottom, and Cross Junction—were green, Port was blue, and Andrews peddler destinations—Corsa and Andrews—were orange. With the incomplete main line, red represented destinations west beyond Great Divide, and black the Tioga Pass interchange to the east. Once the main was completed, John planned to use red and black to signify westbound and eastbound through trips out of Great Divide, around the whole loop, and back again—simulating across-the-division traffic from connecting railroads or adjoining divisions.

These colors were used as codes on the tabs which rode on the cars. "Skate" tabs had little bent-over feet or shortened pins with projecting heads on either side to hold them astraddle a roofwalk. They could also ride atop tank cars or log loads, or inside open-top cars. The H tab was a refinement

of the skate; it looked like a short girder section with flanges to hold it on a roofwalk. The L tab was only for open-tops, and provided a convenient handle for turning. Washer tabs were for tank cars and flatcars with or without loads. A short, unobtrusive pin was mounted on the car or load to hold the washer in place. All tabs had pinheads or short bits of wire staple inside them so they could be picked up with a magnet. The tabs stayed with the cars, and were arranged to require handling (turning over) only at accessible locations on the layout.

The tab cycle. —— Each side of every tab had two blocks of color, one larger than the other. To interpret the destinations the operators followed this sequence: big, little, turn; big, little, turn. Suppose that at Port the yard operator received a boxcar with a tab showing big blue and little yellow. Knowing that blue is Port's color and that the car goes to the big color destination first, he would know it is for delivery at Port. Since Port had many industries, there is a letter code to designate a particular spur, say "BY." If the operator couldn't remember that letter code, he would check the schematic sketch at the control board to find that BY means boatyard, and deliver the car there.

The next time the yard operator got around to working the boatyard spur the little color would tell where the car was going next. By rule a car was supposed to remain spotted after delivery for at least 12 hours. All cars were considered ready to move at the start of each session, so it wasn't hard to keep track of the 12-hour spotting rule in your head. The little color, remember, is yellow, which means the car should be included in fast freight 35 out of Port, because this is a boxcar. Cars for Gorre, "yellow cars," go at the head end of the through freight for easy setout there.

At Gorre the branchline engineer would see the big blue-little yellow tab on one of the boxcars set out by train 35. He would know it had come from Port, so he would ignore the blue destination. If the little yellow code had an "L" code for the Gorre lumberyard, he would spot the car there. Twelve hours (or more) later the Gorre branch engineer would pull the boxcar from the lumberyard spur, see that it has been at its yellow, little color, destination, and know that it is time to turn the tab over. Suppose the other side showed big green and little black. Green, you'll recall, is for the Gorre peddler, so the next time the peddler left Gorre eastbound our boxcar would be in the consist.

On the Gorre and Andrews peddlers the letter codes had to designate both the town and the spur. Thus "Tb" meant the team track/logging spur at Sowbelly, "Tq" was for the team track at Squawbottom, and "CJ" was for the interchange at Cross Junction. Let's say the big code on our boxcar was a green Tq, so the Gorre peddler would set it out on the Squawbottom team track. The next time the Gorre peddler got back to Squawbottom it would be running westbound, and the engineer would see the little black code. This would mean that the boxcar should now head east to connect with the interchange train at Port. Even if 12 hours had passed or a new session had begun since the car was set out, the engineer would leave the car to be picked up by the next eastbound peddler.

The eastbound would take the car to Port, and the Port yardmaster would see that the car was coming from the green train, the Gorre peddler. He would skip the big green code to read the little black, and sort the car into the next TP interchange train. In due course the interchange would take the car up to Cold Shoulder and return it to Port, where the cycle would begin again.

The four-destination tab cycle might be spread over several operating sessions, and this, combined with about 200 cars following their individual cycles, made the repetition unnoticeable to the operators. If John felt that a car's pattern was becoming too obvious, he might swap its tab with one from a similar car, but this behind-the-scenes fiddling was done only between operating sessions. During operation, switching tabs instead of cars would have been cheating.

With so many cars following so many different patterns, the general flow of cars was unpredictable from session to session. A couple of weeks might go by when few cars would come into Port destined for local industries, and the yard operator there would have time to look around and see how the rest of the railroad was running. These lulls preceded storms, however, and the night would soon come when all the cars in the world would roll into Port with blue tabs.

Perry Jenkins tells of his experiences with car flow while working the Andrews peddler: "When I first started working Andrews, I found that it was easy to take the cars out because the trip to Port was downgrade all the way. So, I was cleaning out Andrews and taking out long trains. I didn't notice that not many cars were coming back.

"But those cars were on a four-week cycle, and four weeks later, 40 cars came up the hill! It was impossible to work that many cars because they used up all the track—there was no room for any switching. That day, John gave me special permission to send some of the cars back to Port without delivering them to their industry destinations. I learned to send down the same number of cars as came up, and had no more difficulties at Andrews."

The random flow of cars made assigning motive power a challenge. One week, train 14 might have 12 cars out of Great Divide, and the following session it could have 23. Or the same train might start out with 14 cars and set out six at Gorre, but pick up 12 there. The Great Divide roundhouse foreman would first check the tonnage of the train out of Great Divide, then check with Gorre to see how many cars would have to be hauled up out of Squawbottom, and finally ask the Port yardmaster how many cars would be coming west on the train's return trip. John described one session when the crew failed to coordinate this properly: "We had a real foul-up a couple of months ago due to lack of checking for estimated pickups before assigning the motive power to a through train. The train left Great Divide with 32 cars pulled by two articulateds, which were rated at 14 cars each on the 3.5 percent grade eastbound to Port. Five cars were to be dropped at Gorre, however, I neglected to estimate the pickups from there. It turned out there were 11 pickups, making a train of 38 cars from Gorre. The crew knew it was in trouble, for when it arrived at Squawbottom it would have to start up the 3.5 percent grade to Port, on schedule but 10 cars overloaded.

"At the bottom of the hill [Squawbottom] we commandeered the way freight loco, sitting on a siding waiting for us to go by, as the best out to lose the least amount of time. This got us over the hill, but when we arrived at Port an incorrect estimate of the train's length by the yard crew aligned it so the train couldn't clear the yard switcher pocket, and the

weight of the train, now on the downgrade, made it impossible to back. It was a mess. By the time another relief engine was obtained we had lost 12 hours, and all the other crews had finished their day's work. A good bit of it was my fault and everyone enjoyed my embarrassment. We have never had more than 32 cars before, so we learned by experience."

The peddlers were not allowed the luxury of double-heading, so if the Gorre-bound peddler had too many cars to get up Sims Loop, it would have to double the hill (break the train apart and take it up the grade in two trips). This was exactly the kind of action John liked, and the kind of decision-making he considered appropriate. The tab system certainly made for more operating variety than systems which provide a planned number of cars for every train.

Operating atmosphere. ——— Once the clock was started the operators all got down to work. Although there was no dispatcher, all cooperated to keep the yards and trains coordinated. Communication was mainly just a matter of talking to each other; there was no telephone system. This may seem too simple for a large railroad with several operators, but most of the time the G.D. crew was fairly close together at the Andrews, Gorre, Great Divide, and West Port panels.

At Port there was a dual-head signal near the Railroad Avenue crossover to govern movements of mainline or Andrews branch trains through the yard. The signal could be seen from the Gorre panel, and it was interlocked with the crossover switches and the mainline electrical blocks. A green light on the upper head allowed mainline trains to enter Port, while a green on the lower head cleared trains off the Andrews line. Once a train arrived in the yard, the West Port engineer controlled the signal with a rotary switch to indicate movements for switching. Green told the engineer at the main panel to pull his engine forward, red to stop, and yellow to back up. With these indications and some simple hand signals, such as bringing the palms together to indicate distance between cars to be coupled, most normal moves through Port, the busiest place on the railroad, could be made without any conversation at all.

Since some talking was required to run the railroad, John didn't mind a certain amount of conversation. He felt that the center of interest at an operating session, however, should be the railroad and not socializing or storytelling. One means he used to control this was to discourage non-operating visitors on Tuesday nights. He was happy to show off the railroad at other times, but he wanted operating nights to be for the operators.

Allan Fenton tells of John's attitude toward excess talk during operation: "We had to learn to watch our railroading very closely and not get into predicaments where we had to talk. With a timetable and established tonnage ratings for the locomotives, the only talk should have concerned the train delays, need for helper engines, and peddler freight movements. John's most frequent warnings were 'Keep your speed down,' and 'Don't push the train, take the block' [meaning the operator had tried to run his train into a track block not electrically assigned to his throttle, and couldn't figure out why it refused to move]."

In January 1971 John showed the crew how much excess chatter they indulged in without realizing it. Crew member Andy Sperandeo relates the details: "Jim Findley and John rigged a small cassette tape recorder behind the lighting valance over Gorre to record us as we ran the railroad. When John played the tape for us after the session, there was a lot of talk that had little to do with operation. We did have ten people on hand that night, two learning new positions, which all contributed to the noise level. Interestingly enough, a great deal of the talk was from the maestro himself operating the Gorre branch—he had a way of swearing continuously not quite under his breath when a car wouldn't couple or in some other way flaunted its independence of his will.

"The lesson was well taken, and when the recorder was played back after the next week's session, there was quite a difference. The main sounds were locomotive gears and the 'thunk' of the rotary relay switch machines. Oh yes, there were a few plaintive cries such as 'Won't you ever let the peddler into Port?' "

This doesn't mean that John wanted operating sessions to be somber and mirthless. He wrote: "This may sound as though model railroading is all serious work with me. Quite to the contrary; I enjoy horsing around, bull sessions, and gaming with trains. It is just during the operation itself that I prefer serious effort. Our operations are very informal, and if something happens, we josh a bit, but not long enough to foul up the operating tempo. We save the storytelling and good fellowship till coffee time."

Andy Sperandeo told me of one of the perils of operating Port: "John had a built-in joke which I was often the victim of. Hidden somewhere below Port was a mechanical laugh box. It was supposedly connected to the West Port controls, but I never did figure out exactly what triggered it. John wanted us to concentrate on doing our best job of railroading, but he didn't want us to take it too seriously."

Nightfall on the G.D. —— John's night lighting effects were another interesting dimension of G.D. operation. The night cycle lasted about six scale hours. It was started and stopped from a switch on the Gorre panel. Andy Sperandeo tells of nightfall: "Sometimes if John was very busy at Gorre it never got dark at all, or if he was distracted after turning the switch on we might have a day with both a night and a long total eclipse. On the average we came close to the prototype ratio of one night every 24 hours.

"The railroad went right on running after dark, which meant that we had to keep reading tabs and switching cars. For this purpose, John provided penlights to use to see the color codes and for hand signals. It wasn't any easier to switch in the dark, but that was part of the challenge. There was a certain realism to using the switch engine's headlight to see which way the next turnout was thrown."

Day or night, operation on the Gorre & Daphetid was an immense and infinitely complex game, engrossing for the operators—the players—and demanding of the railroad and its equipment—the board and the tokens. More than that, realistic operation was the goal John had set out to achieve when he planned the railroad so thoroughly in 1953. Save for the great bridge over Devil's Gulch and a few feet of track, he fully realized that goal. Just a few days after John's death in January 1973, Allan Fenton wrote to me: "We all knew he only planned one day at a time in his life, but planned many years ahead for his railroad, and followed his plan. The last day's discussion, before he died, was how, by completing the last bridge, the traffic flow through Port would change. Maybe it would not be the bottleneck it had become."

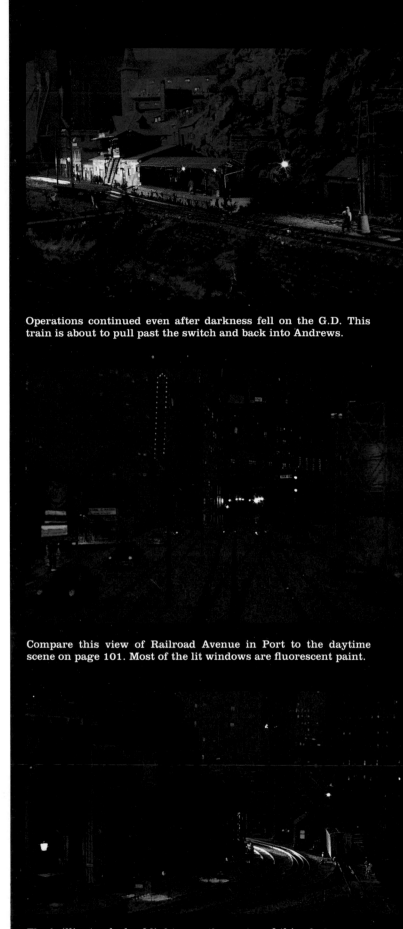

Operations continued even after darkness fell on the G.D. This train is about to pull past the switch and back into Andrews.

Compare this view of Railroad Avenue in Port to the daytime scene on page 101. Most of the lit windows are fluorescent paint.

The brilliant splash of light near the center of this photo means that the switcher is on its way back to the East Port yard office.

Whit's Tower, left, dominated the breathtaking nighttime cityscape at Port.

Austin Street station, like most G.D. structures, included full night-lighting effects.

With her rods and drivers a blur, Gorre & Daphetid number 25, one of the line's smaller locomotives, crosses the Howe truss bridge at French Gulch.

"Most model railroads are top-heavy with locomotives, and mine is no exception."

The G.D. roster

IN LATER YEARS the Gorre & Daphetid roster numbered about 30 engines, a mix of ancient, old, and relatively modern steam locomotives. While John intentionally designed the railroad to exclude heavy modern steam power, his favorite engines all had short, large-diameter boilers, low drivers, and an overall "husky" look. He was not a locomotive collector, and rarely did he have more locomotives than he needed. After buying 2-6-6-2 number 39, his thirtieth standard gauge engine, he wrote to Jim Findley in 1968: "This, I hope, will be my last locomotive, but I doubt it. Even now, two or three have to be taken off the pike for lack of parking space."

John never concerned himself with the prototype of an engine when choosing it for the G.D.; his criteria were that the engine would look right on his railroad and run well. Let's take a look at what he chose.

The G.D. locomotive stud. —— The G.D.'s early locomotives, like those of many prototype railroads, were of limited usefulness when the road grew larger. Once John developed his permanent concept for the G.D., each locomotive acquired was intended for a specific service. John scolded me once for suggesting that he might like to have a 4-4-0 that I had been given: "My railroad is not an 'old time' pike. Why did you think I'd want another 4-4-0?" he asked.

The largest wheel arrangements on the G.D. roster were a 2-8-4, a 2-10-2, and several articulateds, but each was a relatively small example of its type. Perhaps most typical of the roster was the beefy 4-10-0 John built for the second, expanded, G.D. All of these larger engines were appropriate for the short trains John liked. By "short trains" he meant trains of ten cars or so with one engine or 16 to 18 cars with a helper engine.

"There is no need for train length to be limited by operating rules with 4 percent ruling grades cropping up at several places," John wrote to his operating round robin friends. "The model can haul about what the prototype can in cars on that kind of grade. No loco I have can haul more than 14 cars up that grade and prototype railroads can't do quite that well. My tonnage ratings are what the locos can do less a safety factor of 10 percent, or one car.

"I agree that train length may be limited more by siding length than by loco ability. That's one reason I prefer middle-size locos over the giants except for a railroad designed for very long trains. A 2-8-0 looks better to me with 15 to 20 cars than a 2-10-2 unless the grades are heavy."

Most of the G.D.'s first locomotives were built from die-cast metal kits, and during the '50s John added several engines made from parts and scratch. Before imported brass engines came along in the mid-1950s the variety of kit locomotives was limited, and one interesting modification John made to several of them was to cut new axle slots in the frame to vary the driver spacing or number of wheels.

When brass locomotives began to be imported in quantity, John favored them for new additions to his roster. He wrote to Jim Findley that it was easier to write an article for MODEL RAILROADER and put the proceeds toward an engine than build the engine himself.

The accompanying Gorre & Daphetid motive power roster was compiled from several lists John had made and from purchase invoices, comments in letters, photos, and caption information. There are mysteries: For instance, I do not know when or where John obtained 2-6-6-2 number 36, but he mentioned it in a letter and he listed it more than once. Also, the roster is not complete for motive power acquired in the 1970s.

Performance improvements. —— John tinkered with every engine to improve its performance. Sliding pickup shoes to ensure better electrical contact were mounted on both sides under locos and tenders, and each engine was modified to run at scale speeds, usually by limiting the motor voltage but in some cases by refitting gears.

When Bob Higgins, author of the locomotive performance reviews in the NMRA *Bulletin*, proposed that model locomotives should run at speeds proportional to their driving wheel diameters for any given voltage, John disagreed. He

Most of the G.D. Line's passenger power was rounded up for this composite portrait near the Cutoff connection at Great Divide.

opposed this idea because locos with different-size drivers then could not be run in the same train. Instead he suggested in a letter to the *Bulletin* that locos run at speeds proportional to voltage regardless of wheel diameter. "I run my trains," he wrote, "at an allowable speed consistent with the territory, and adjust the throttle accordingly. I really care not how fast they run at 12 volts, unless at this maximum voltage they are not able to haul their trains at acceptable speeds for the grade."

About engine weight, another of his pet topics, John wrote: "The balancing of weight over the drivers is important. I would prefer to keep an engine well balanced than to get more traction by loading one end over what can be put at the other. Balancing can usually be done very nicely by pouring in lead or Cerrobend [a low-melting-point alloy]."

John may have had a PFM Mikado, engine 40, in mind, when he continued: "As brass locos usually come, they are quite light and not able to pull as many cars as the prototype

GORRE & DAPHETID LOCOMOTIVES

Road Number	Wheel Arrangement	Acquired or Built	Cars Pulled	Top Speed	Notes
1	2-2-0	1947	0		Named *Charles Rush* in honor of a member of the local model railroad club. Built from a Strombecker wood kit, had no motor. Metal wheels added to pick up current for headlight. Retired in 1949 after John built No. 2, a much finer model.
2	4-2-0	1948	0		Named *C.D. Grandt*. Had 42″ drivers, 20″ lead wheels. Length 17′-8″, with tender 29′-10″. A dummy, it required a helper in the form of a motorized gondola behind it.
4	4-4-0	1951	3	40 mph	Historic passenger loco, a Mantua *General*. John did not care for the 4-4-0 type after enlarging the layout because the models had little pulling ability.
6	Heisler geared	1958	7	15 mph	Logging and switching. For a while this engine was numbered 8. United brand brass import.
7	Shay geared	1957	7	15 mph	Logging and switching. United brass import.
8	4-4-0	1947	4	45 mph	Named the *Sergeant Ennis*. Assembled from a Mantua *Belle of the '80s* brass kit.
9	0-4-0T	1946	6	25 mph	The first G.D. locomotive. It carried the number 98 and was used mostly in peddler service. On the new G.D. as number 9 it did yard switching. Re-detailed in 1950. "For its weight," John said, "this engine is the best performer on the system."
10	0-4-0T	1965	5-6	25 mph	Yard goat and switcher. Made by Sakura.
12	0-6-0	1950	6	25 mph	First used as a mainline peddler but replaced by a 2-8-0 and diverted to switching in Great Divide on the old G.D. Roundhouse 0-6-0 kit.
13	Organic switcher	1951	2	1 mph	Named *Emma*, stegosaur found in woods near tracks. An amiable creature, the company put it to work switching cars, rescuing derailments, and pulling stumps. Consumed lichen for fuel. Unlike other motive power, had to be steered along the track but had the advantage of running around cars without needing a passing track. Worked equally well on narrow gauge. Did not learn to use the ash pit.
14	Railcar	1950	0		The *President's car*. This standard gauge touring car with railroad wheels was similar to narrow gauge number 6, the *Ruptured Duck*. Scratchbuilt, including the motor.
15	0-8-0	1958	0	20 mph	Switcher (before 1962, number 5). Transfer switching, snowplow pusher, and maintenance-of-way service. Parts-built in G.D. shops.
25	2-6-0	1956	6	35 mph	Light freight duty. Used around the mines and in branch service. "Although converted to coal, a spark arrester is added as it runs through heavily wooded areas." This engine and number 12 were backshopped by the G.D. from Roundhouse 0-6-0 switchers. A new axle slot was cut into the rear of the frame and new side rods added. Pilot was extended to allow for pilot truck. Tender scratchbuilt.
26	2-8-0	1957	10	35 mph	Medium freight. Used in peddler service along main line. Usually fitted with a short tender so it can use the turntable at Gorre. Front of tender is low because of the full load of coal. United brand, Union Pacific prototype.
27	2-8-0	1957	11-12	35 mph	Helper service; has tender booster engine. United brand, AT&SF prototype.
28	2-8-0	1961	10	35 mph	Medium freight. United AT&SF prototype. In 1961 John and I drove about California visiting modelers. I sent him this loco afterward as a thank you for the wear and tear on his car.
29	2-8-0	1962-1967	9-10	35 mph	Medium freight. United B&O prototype. Sound unit.
34	4-10-0	1952	13	30 mph	Heavy helper service. This was the epitome of G.D. motive power. Built from parts, including a Varney Reading 2-8-0 boiler, Mantua 50″ drivers, Varney *Casey Jones* cylinders, and a scratchbuilt tender.

on, say, a 3 or 4 percent grade. The prototype would be good for 12 cars at about 25 miles per hour. After pouring in some weight, and in this case I didn't put in the maximum, the engine pulls a respectable 13 cars easily, which is what I need for a 12-car rating with my 10 percent safety factor."

John used melted lead to weight his locomotives, and he developed a way to fill a boiler with lead without things coming unsoldered. "After breaking in a brass engine I always take out the loco weight and then fill the boiler with lead unless it's a large loco, then complete filling may be too much

weight. Beside improving tractive force, the solid lead fill will reduce the soundboard effect of the shell. Be sure to install the headlight wires first. I use hard insulated telephone wire, which is not even scorched by the heat. This is only through the boiler. The bulb wires are soldered to the end.

"If the boiler is wrapped in wet rags and poured about one-half inch at a time, no soldering will come undone. I have even poured painted boilers for friends without hurting the paint job, but then the heat transfer to wet rags is slower, so I reduce the amount of each pour a little."

Road Number	Wheel Arrangement	Acquired or Built	Cars Pulled	Top Speed	Notes
35	0-6-6-0	1962			Used in helper service. Modified in 1965 from a Pacific Fast Mail Sierra 2-6-6-2 with new dome and sandboxes, new pilot, firebox modified for coal. PFM tender from an 0-8-0.
36	2-6-6-2	unknown			Listed in 1967 as custom built. A helper engine. Omitted from equipment list in 1968.
37	2-6-6-2	1956-1960	13	20 mph	Prototype was the first American 2-6-6-2, built for Great Northern. Imported by Austin.
38	2-6-6-2	1960	13	30 mph	Slow freight. This engine does much work around mines and with ore trains. The weathering is redder than for most other engines. United Sierra.
39	2-6-6-2	1968			Heavy freight. John added weight, wanting it to pull 16 or 20 cars "as would the prototype" on the 4 percent grades. United, C&O prototype. Sound system added in 1972. Also had smoke unit.
40	2-8-2	1963	13-14	40 mph	Fast freight. Along with the other Mikado, number 42, and 4-10-0 number 34, one of the three most powerful haulers on the system. United, AT&SF prototype.
42	2-8-2	1952	13	40 mph	Fast freight. Remodeled in 1960. Sandbox, cab, superheater altered using HObbyline Berkshire parts. Mantua Mikado kit. Tender scratchbuilt except for trucks.
43	2-10-2	1970			John mentioned this engine twice in notes and letters. Engine number, date purchased not certain. It probably would have been a United, AT&SF prototype.
45	2-8-4	1961	14	40 mph	Fast passenger, through mainline service. Body modified from the John English (HObbyline) plastic Nickel Plate Berkshire. Mechanism is Sims Lab, made for that kit. Metal trucks used, trailing truck shortened. Boiler shortened 2 scale feet.
48	4-6-0	1962-1967	5	45 mph	Light passenger. United, Canadian Pacific prototype.
49	4-6-0	(1952) 1956	7	45 mph	Light passenger and mixed service. A Varney *Casey Jones* kit which was sent to John for the Varney ad photos. Only after 1953 did John consider it a G.D. engine. United tender from UP 2-8-0. Had smoke unit.
50	4-6-2	1957	10	50 mph	Medium-heavy Pacific for passenger service. John said this engine was the poorest puller on the system considering its weight. Originally number 52 but renumbered after 1962. Modified from a Varney Economy Pacific. Boiler shortened near the cab and inside-bearing trailing truck substituted. Bowser tender. Painted green.
56	4-6-2	1958	9	50 mph	First-class passenger service. This is the railroad's showpiece. The boiler jacket was painted Mandarin Red, the running gear, smoke box, firebox, and cab roof were silver-gray. A Bowser NYC class K3 Pacific with United AT&SF 2-8-0 tender.
60	Gas-electric	1950	1	60 mph	Gas-electric car for mail and passenger service. Has controls at each end so it can run in either direction if not pulling its wood trailer. "Rebuilt in the G.D. shops from an interurban car body." Scratchbuilt except for the trucks, pilot, and couplers. Originally number 34.
101	4-6-4	1949			A Gilbert American Flyer locomotive. Odd, "Rock Island" style Vanderbilt tender. Although it couldn't run on the original G.D. curves, it was obtained for mainline operation on the expanded G.D. No longer listed in 1967.

DEVIL'S GULCH & HELENGON LOCOMOTIVES (HOn3)

Road Number	Wheel Arrangement	Acquired or Built	Cars Pulled	Top Speed	Notes
1	0-6-0T	1950			Mechanism built by Cliff Grandt. Stolen from the workbench, still unfinished, about 1962 when a group was visiting.
3	2-4-0T	1949	4		Built on a Lindsey-Kemtron mechanism, following drawings of three different Porter locomotives. Front and rear headlights work.
6	Railbus	1949			Converted touring car extended to have 5 bench seats with canopy over rear seat for first-class passengers. Small platform for freight at rear. Locally known as the *Ruptured Duck*. Cliff Grandt made a small motor. Required a push to get it started.

Notes: Car ratings are on 4 percent grade. Speed is on level track. Passenger engines are rated in freight cars pulled.

Exchangeable tenders. —— If you study his photos carefully, you'll see that John swapped tenders freely among his locomotives to vary their appearance. He wrote: "For some years I have equipped all my locos with a standard drawbar so any tender can be coupled to any loco. The drawbars are arranged so that any combination of engine to tender will have a prototype distance between engine and tender. The locomotive carries its number, but the tender has the railroad name and herald."

Whether they were coal, wood, or oil types, tenders had to couple close to the engine. In a 1963 letter, John wrote: "It's the cab overhang that I, too, most object to, but even then, a scale coupling distance between loco and tender is practical if the loco-tender drawbar is designed correctly. I'm a bug on this ever since riding and looking out between the tender and loco on the McCloud River Lumber Co. By sheer chance I was leaning back into the cab instead of out, and as we came around a curve my knuckles touched the tender handrails. Now I won't have the engine and tender more than a scale distance apart. All my engines, including my Berk-

All the early G.D. and D.G.& H. motive power was spotted near the Gorre enginehouse for this 1953 photo. The large engine ahead of 4-10-0 No. 34 is No. 101, John's modified American Flyer HO Hudson, and the small unpainted engine next to the gas-electric is D.G.& H. No. 1, which was later stolen by a visitor.

shire, are so spaced, and all run on my 26″ radius curves."

"I've never found it difficult," John wrote to a correspondent in 1964, "to insulate tender bodies from their trucks, then use pickup independent of the tender body for loco pickup. This allows a prototype distance between engine and tender without any danger of short circuits from occasional touching of the handrails on a tight curve."

Lighting, sound systems, and paint. —— By 1970, all G.D. engines had been equipped with diode-drop constant lighting for the headlight and tender, and red firebox illumination. As sound systems for model locomotives began to appear in the late '60s John tried several of them. In October 1971 he wrote to Findley: "Put a Modeltronics sound unit in a tender and think it pretty good. Not too easy to install, but I like it. It requires no change in the electrical system, and uses power from a 9-volt transistor radio battery as well as

(Left) Both No. 12 and No. 25 were built from Roundhouse die-cast 0-6-0 kits. Number 12 was modified only slightly, but No. 25 was converted to a 2-6-0 by moving one driver set back under the cab and extending the pilot deck to accommodate a two-wheel pony truck.

(Above) Number 42, an extensively redetailed Mantua Mikado, was one of the G.D.'s most sure-footed engines. Shay No. 7, at right, often served as the branchline switcher at Gorre. (Below) As another locomotive rolls off the Great Divide turntable, 2-6-6-2 No. 39 dumps her fire in the ashpit. The 39 was a C&O-prototype engine, a handsome model, but for some reason that John never managed to uncover, a poor puller.

A hot summer evening at Great Divide terminal finds seven G.D. locomotives in the open-air service area, and yet another rolling onto the vacant track. The heavy weathering John applied to his motive power did a great deal to establish the G.D.'s hard-working character.

the track power. The sound goes up and down automatically with the speed of the loco."

Later, in 1972, John changed his mind about the battery-powered systems and wrote to John Schedler of Modeltronics: "I'm fairly convinced that I don't want any more units with batteries, even though I can get an air pump effect only with them. I just don't have much faith that the batteries won't leak and cause a real mess as they have in tape recorders and such."

Many of today's modelers will be appalled to learn how John painted his locomotives. For starters, he never used an airbrush: "All painting is done by hand brush using flat oil paint such as Pactra enamel. I prefer two thin coats to one heavy one as this seems to lessen the obstruction of fine detail. The boilers are cleaned thoroughly before painting by lightly scrubbing with weak acid and then rinsing. Black locomotive paint is mixed to the desired color, usually 70 percent black, 25 percent white, and 5 percent red." John

(Above) While Ten-Wheeler No. 49 waits in the hole at the Austin Street station, 2-8-0 No. 29 rolls past with a westbound freight. John's roster included four chunky Consolidations similar to No. 29, making that wheel arrangement one of his favorites. (Below) Numbers 35 and 38 started life as nearly identical Pacific Fast Mail "Sierra" 2-6-6-2's, but John converted No. 35 to an 0-6-6-0 by removing the lead and trailing trucks and shortening the pilot deck. Both engines were especially fine runners, and the G.D. operators liked them.

(Above and top) John's bobtailed On3 combine and HO sheep car were among his finest individual rolling stock models. The matching HO gauge combine beside the On3 car was built for the Gorre & Daphetid by John's good friend Bill Hoffman.

(Left) As 2-6-6-2 No. 37 battles upgrade toward Port with drag freight tonnage, "Gasatronic" car No. 60 rolls passengers and mail for Andrews across French Gulch. This part of the layout was one of John's favorites for photographing locomotives and rolling stock.

added that he varied colors from engine to engine, and that the principal thing to remember about weathering was not to overdo it.

"I almost always run a loco for a while in regular operation to get the mechanism worked to good performance both before painting and before adding delicate details that might be damaged during disassembly, such as bell cords. I paint all that I can see with the loco on the track, but I don't bother to paint places that cannot be seen."

Hands off! —— Operators, not to mention visitors, were not allowed to handle G.D. equipment. If an engine derailed or stalled, the operator called John, who moved it or made the required adjustment. John explained: "Many people do not know how to nudge a stalled train and will push on the headlight or leave a greasy fingerprint on the cab roof. On this

railroad no one puts a derailed loco back on the track but me. First I want to know why it derailed and to check the track or loco for repairs and second, different locos should be handled differently. This doesn't happen enough to be a chore for me, and it keeps me on maintenance."

Even John avoided lifting cars completely clear of the track unless absolutely necessary, which brings up the tale of the great Helengon wreck. Don Mitchell wrote me about "the time John spilled most of a 20-plus car train into the bed of Squawbottom Creek while attempting to negotiate the 'U' turn through Helengon Gap at the Andrews end of Squawbottom. As I recall the incident," Don continues, "I was operating the Daphetid branch while another military type from a local base was running the through freight on the main line. As he pulled his train out of Squawbottom and around the bend, he suffered a minor derailment which he requested me

Thundering upgrade around Sims Loop, G.D. No. 39, the road's largest and most modern locomotive, hauls a through freight westbound toward Gorre. All G.D. engines had constant-brightness headlights, and most had a glowing red bulb in the firebox as well. Number 39 even had a smoke unit, which John didn't often use because it made the track dirty.

to rerail. (At that time John was still fairly restrictive about who could handle cars on the layout and I was allowed to if I used extreme care. Bill Corsa was the only one, beside John, allowed to rerail a locomotive.)

"After the cars were rerailed, the operator commenced to pull forward with his train. We noted several empty log bunks near the middle of the train were starting to lift their wheels from the outer rail and tilt to the inside of the curve. The throttle was shut off immediately, the train reversed, and slack taken. This allowed the log bunk wheels to settle back on the rail. We tried again with the same results and then called John for advice.

"John's first directions were to double the hill. [That means leave half the train behind and come back for it later.] Then he changed his mind and said that because we were running late he would run the train until it got past the curve. John took over the throttle and v-e-r-y slowly eased the train forward. As the train moved, the log cars tilted slowly—less than before but still lifting from the outer rail.

"It looked like John would succeed. Then, for whatever reason, disaster! Car after car tumbled into the gorge. John's reaction was immediate, vocal, loud, and colorful. Several cars were the worse for wear and retired from the consist. The log bunks were lifted out of the train and recoupled at the rear of the train.

"John moved to the workshop with the bad order cars. The rest of us went back to operating, albeit in a considerably more restrained atmosphere than before. It seemed that John was particularly gracious at the coffee session afterwards."

Visiting power—including a diesel. —— While John preferred to use his own engines in photos, any operator with a steam locomotive in good condition could run it on the G.D. Joe Cain and Bill Corsa both ran their 2-6-6-2 engines on the line, and Bill also had a Shay, a Heisler, and a Climax locomotive in regular service. The Climax was used mostly in John's Timesaver switching game.

While I was discussing this practice with Jim Findley, he

Shiny No. 56, the G.D. superintendent's pride and joy, highballs across French Gulch with the road's mandarin-red first-class passenger train. This is one of several panned action photos John made of moving engines by attaching a trammel-like device to the train which rotated the camera on its tripod as the train moved by.

pointed out that a typical model railroad is in a sense "tuned" to its locomotive roster, and vice versa. By this he meant that gradually the track kinks on a layout that derail one of the locomotives are eliminated, and pilot trucks that balk at switches are replaced or adjusted until few performance flaws remain. Because John was meticulous in his maintenance, the situation existed that while his locomotives gave perfect performances on the layout, visitors' engines might not do as well.

Findley also told me of a mischievous trick John played once or twice. When a new visitor to the G.D. brought an engine to run, John would select several of his heaviest, most sluggish cars to couple behind it, without telling the unsuspecting guest. Then, when the engine couldn't haul the comparatively short string of cars up the grade, John would say: "Well, I'm surprised. I was thinking of buying one of those engines, but it looks like it doesn't have much pulling power!"

Because the G.D. represented a period before diesel loco-

motives were developed for mainline service, model diesels were rarely seen on the property. I was talking about this with the G.D. operators, and Joe Cain added: "Darrell Harbin was the only operator that was allowed to run a diesel on John's railroad."

"How come you were allowed to?" I asked, and Darrell answered: "I had a TR6, a powered 'cow and calf,' and I used it in heavy switching at Great Divide. Whenever John would take pictures, he removed it. On the next operating night I'd have to hunt for it in the back room. I don't think he ever took a photograph of it. When Bill Corsa moved away, I took over his peddler run and used the TR6 on that."

Rolling stock notes. —— The rolling stock roster on the G.D. was every bit as varied as the locomotive stud, if not more so. Included in the nearly 200 cars were swaybacked wood cars with truss rods, streamlined passenger cars, and just about everything in between. Other than that it run well and look like typical railroad equipment, in later years John did not give much thought to the car fleet on the G.D.

This wasn't always the case. When John started model railroading in the late 1940s he built several exquisite cars, at least one of them a contest winner. His ¼″ scale narrow gauge combine earned the Best of Show award at the 1950 Pacific Coast Region NMRA convention in San Diego. John also scratchbuilt a superb double-deck sheep car, attempting to hold all dimensions as close to exact scale as possible, including the wheels. He even dipped a brass brake wheel in nitric acid to reduce it to scale dimensions.

Most, if not all, of the cars John built when he first started model railroading were still operating in 1972, 25 years later, and if you study the photos carefully you'll be able to spot many of them on all three G.D. layouts. The same is true of most of John's early structure models.

Trucks and couplers. —— Because John had always been interested in closer-to-scale track and wheels, dozens of different trucks and wheel designs ran—and ran well— on the Gorre & Daphetid. Interestingly enough, John wasn't enthusiastic about free-rolling Delrin trucks when they appeared. He wrote: "I don't want 'em. Too many spurs on my railroad have some grade and I don't like putting something under the wheels to hold the cars. Also, a car which has the ability to roll on a 1 percent grade allows for adding only about one car in eight on my 4 percent grades, compared to cars that require a 2 percent grade to roll. Free-rolling cars also push on the loco going downgrade, making the engine want to buck at slow speeds. No, I'd just as soon have wheels that have a little braking action. My locos pull the same number of cars on a 4 percent grade as the prototype engines do...My cabooses have wipers on their axles. This dampens train rolling and also provides a good light pickup."

Whenever fellow modelers argued that all cars should weigh approximately the same for good operation, John disagreed: "My cars are not of uniform weight, just as with the prototype. However, just as with the prototype, when a train is long, light cars and long cars are put on the rear. In heavy mountain country the timetables spell this out."

The G.D. used Baker couplers, an early automatic design that may not have looked much like a prototype coupler, but which worked reliably. They uncoupled mechanically when the lower portions of the couplers, below the hoop and hook, were lifted by retractable ramps between the rails. There were both electrically and mechanically actuated ramps on the layout. The couplers could also be uncoupled anywhere by inserting a curved strip of metal, called a "spoon," between the cars to lift the uncoupling pins.

John had plenty to say about couplers. "The prime importance of any coupler is to work dependably. I have an aversion to fixed ramps, and prefer the kinds where you push a button to activate a ramp, whether it be a magnet or lift type. I also dislike the slack principle which requires a backward movement off the ramp after a gentle coupling. Admittedly, dropping a car while moving forward is un-prototype due to the need for slack to lift the pin, but they don't use automatic coupling yet, either."

John modified all his Baker couplers by removing the spring which held the coupling hook in its down position, making it much easier to couple onto a car. "It is extremely important to me," John wrote, "to be able to move up to a single car on a spur and pick it up without moving it, or at least

Rugged Robinson Cliff is the setting as Heisler No. 6 struggles mightily against the tail end of a log train headed upgrade to Port. On the track below, Consolidation No. 27 drifts downgrade with a string of empty ore cars bound for Squawbottom Mine. The "Butler Mines" ore cars are some of the first rolling stock John built.

using no more than a prototype nudge. This automatically prohibits the types of permanent mechanical uncoupling ramps over which you must shove the car 15 or 20 scale feet before pulling forward. I require a coupler with a light coupling performance."

Maintaining the fleet. —— Because the cars were the pieces in the G.D. operation game, John valued mechanical perfection much more than prototype fidelity. He wrote: "Nothing shows up poor mechanical performance as will a tight timecard. It shows up personal incapabilities in the same way. It pinpoints needed maintenance and instruction. It is to operation as a photo is to a scale model."

Andy Sperandeo writes of how maintenance problems were spotted during an operating session. "A system of tagging cars identified problems for correction. John kept small precut squares of red electrical tape on the back of an NMRA standards gauge, and when a car derailed we tagged the end that had come off the track with a red square on the roof. When a car collected three squares it was placed on the workbench for repair or adjustment. A similar procedure with yellow tags was used for coupler malfunctions...The first thing we did [at the start of an operating session] was to check all the track cleaner cars. These were regular house-type freight cars with holes drilled in their floors to loosely accept nails glued to pads of Masonite (the kind with one rough side) which slid along the rails between the trucks. The pads simply floated, rough side down, without springs or weights for additional pressure. There were several of these cars and they simply circulated in normal freight service. The only effect they had on train makeup was that they were counted as two cars for tonnage purposes."

That completes our survey of John's railroad. Next, we'll learn a bit more about John himself, especially his humorous side.

Scenes like this one from Bill McClanahan's book, SCENERY FOR MODEL RAILROADS, did much to establish John Allen's reputation as the dean of model railroaders.

"The fact that I may half hide a full-sized replica of a snake in my scenery, or pose a much-oversized miniature alligator pursuing an unconcerned fisherman in a boat, is there because this amuses me, not that I don't know better."

WHAT WAS IT LIKE to know this fellow John Allen? When I interviewed many of John's friends, I found that no two of them saw John quite the same way. Certainly he was a friendly man, and almost anyone who got to know him became a good friend. By 1965 he received and tried to answer almost 200 letters per year, and he kept up personal correspondence with a number of model railroading friends, some of them overseas. Although he preferred to know in advance if someone wished to visit, he almost never turned down a polite request to see the Gorre & Daphetid.

The conversationalist. —— You'll remember that John was a bachelor. People who live by themselves are often great talkers when they are with others, and this was surely true of him. I remember one occasion when he, Ken Barnhart, and I spent all night discussing model railroading at Ken's house. We couldn't stop.

Cliff Robinson recalled how John could engross himself in a conversation: "I was talking with a bunch at a model railroad convention in Chicago when one of the fellows said that he had gone up to John Allen and introduced himself. He complained, 'John just ignored me.' I replied, 'Well, I know John, and I'll bet you a dollar that he was talking with his hand in his hip pocket.' (A habit of his when he was deep in a conversation.) 'John didn't intend to be rude, but he was probably so enthralled with the sound of his own voice that he wasn't even conscious of his surroundings!' The following year I met this same fellow at another meet in the East. We

The Wizard

# of Monterey

Who else would think of adding a subway to a model railroad city, and then do it? Mirrors added the illusion of depth here, and upon hearing the approaching train, many visitors waited for it to appear. Of course, it never did.

were walking over to get a drink and bumped into John on the way. I started to introduce the fellow, but John said, 'Oh, I met you in Chicago last year. Can I buy you a drink?'"

John read extensively on many subjects, and he remembered what he read. Earl Flaws told me how John impressed his wife on his first visit to their home: "No matter what the topic, John could speak on it intelligently. My wife is an opera buff, and she found that John knew all about the current highly regarded opera performers."

John loved to argue, and it didn't matter which side you took, he could take the other. Conversation was a game of wits with him, and one of his tricks was to bombard his adversary with question after question until he found one the opponent could not answer. Once his psychological victory was won, John might quietly admit you were right after all—it was important to him to be fair—and I never remember him maneuvering just to save face. If you were indeed right, he wasn't stubborn about the viewpoint he'd espoused.

That's not to say John couldn't get irritated. One thing he didn't like was discourtesy, and he was always very courteous himself. He didn't like to boast, nor did he like to hear others boast. This occasionally put John in a difficult position, because while many model railroaders practically idolized him, a few others resented the publicity his railroad received and the acclaim showered on him. Once, when I hadn't printed a feature on the Gorre & Daphetid in MODEL RAILROADER for more than two years, John published an article in *Railroad Model Craftsman* and I got not one but several letters complaining of "too much John Allen in MODEL RAILROADER."

The Wizard. ——— One of John's admirers dubbed him "The Wizard of Monterey," and that title stayed with him for the rest of his life. Sometimes his fame embarrassed John. Once, when he was registering at a motel in Sacramento the desk clerk, who as luck would have it was a model railroader, saw John's name and asked "Are you *the* John Allen?" Sensing John's uneasiness, Cliff Grandt then proceeded to walk backwards down the aisleway bowing and kowtowing to John all the way. All John could say was "get away, get away."

As I said, John didn't like to boast, but he did have confidence in his own modeling practices, particularly in the areas of coloring, lighting, photography, and operation. He was always willing to tell others how he achieved his results, but he never implied that his personal choices were best.

In all the years I knew John I do not recall him ever claiming to have been the first to do something, even though he could have—for a number of things. Boasting was not his way of getting satisfaction. He did, however, enjoy it when people enjoyed something he'd done. One of the ways he derived that satisfaction was to play a little trick by tucking surprises here and there and waiting for his operators and visitors to discover them. The longer you took to discover the novelty, the more pleased he was that he had outsmarted you for a while. No words of praise were needed for that sort of satisfaction.

Some creative people are jealous of other creators and will give them credit only grudgingly; this was not at all true of John. While he liked to receive credit for his own accomplishments, he never complained when others took his ideas, published them, and didn't even mention where the ideas

One of the most memorable photo stories about the Gorre & Daphetid was a special fan trip conducted in 1971 for Railroad Model Craftsman magazine. Here, G.D. gas-electric car No. 60 leaves Eagle's Nest with publisher Hal Carstens' gaudy visiting private car.

really came from. John himself was very careful to credit other modelers when he got a good idea from them. And if you asked his opinion about something that seemed competitive with one of his methods, such as a different way to create momentum effects with throttles or to make model trees,

John would simply admit that he hadn't tried the other method so couldn't say which was better.

The Great Pooh-Bah. —— John was a big man, and somewhere along the line a model railroad friend gave him the

Model railroads weren't the only things that interested John. After trying unsuccessfully to persuade others in our model railroad tour group to ride this merry-go-round at the Munich Oktoberfest, he gamely decided to ride it by himself.

Two of John's Timesaver switching layouts connected back-to-back made a game that pairs of railroaders could play as two-man teams. (Above) Well-known modelers Whit Towers (left) and Leighton Keeling, both seated, tackle the problem. Meanwhile, John (left, standing) and Jim Findley look on, heckle the players a bit, and wait for their turn. Photo by Linn Westcott. (Below) This is the plan for the dual Timesaver. It differs from John's first design only in the turnout that goes to the connecting track between the two boards.

nickname of "The Great Pooh-Bah." He didn't often admit it, but he liked the nickname, in fact, he liked it well enough that he had calling cards printed. Cliff Robinson tells of an incident in Little Rock, Arkansas, when a waiter saw one of these cards. Later, while John was out of the dining room, the others at the table told the waiter that they were transferring John from one insane asylum to another. The waiter steered clear of John for the rest of the meal.

Once or twice some of the G.D. operators even picketed an NMRA banquet with signs, some for and some against The Great Pooh-Bah. The nickname, by the way, did not imply that John was haughty or ostentatious. He was very frugal, even in later years when he could easily have lived quite lavishly, had he wanted to. Cliff Robinson told me: "When he was by himself, he was not a great spender, but more than once I saw him quietly pick up the check at an expensive restaurant where some of the fellows in the group might have been hard-pressed to settle up for the bill."

The appreciative visitor. —— In the '50s and '60s John made many trips around the country visiting other model railroaders. He always caught on quickly as to how a particular railroad ran, and he became an authority on the convenience—or lack of it—of various kinds of control panels. One of his greatest pleasures was to attend some of the NMRA national and regional conventions, as long as they were not held in hot states during the summer.

John joined my wife Harriet and me on our model railroad tours to Europe in 1969 and 1971. On these tours John was fairly quiet, often off to the side of the group studying something that particularly interested him. He was careful not to walk too fast (because of his heart), but otherwise he participated in everything we did.

When visiting layouts on these tours it was clear that John saw more features of interest in every model railroad than anyone else. Afterward, he could tell you every detail of how the builder laid the track, built the scenery, structures, or rolling stock, and often he deduced how the wiring was done. He was quick to show his appreciation of any area where the other modeler had done a good job, too. Cliff Robinson said: "You'd be looking at the layout and taking in all the sights, and you'd think to yourself: 'Well John has come and said hello to this man and hasn't taken the trouble to look at his railroad.' But when you got back out to the car, John could tell you more about that railroad than you'd seen for yourself!"

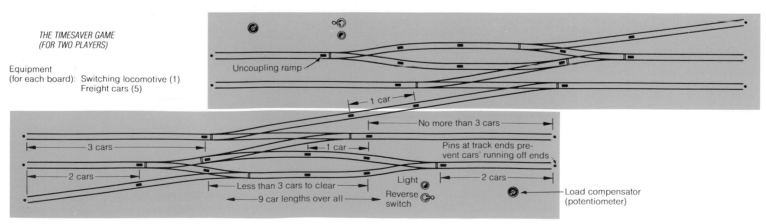

THE TIMESAVER GAME
(FOR TWO PLAYERS)

Equipment
(for each board): Switching locomotive (1)
Freight cars (5)

Uncoupling ramp

1 car

No more than 3 cars

3 cars

1 car

Pins at track ends prevent cars' running off ends

2 cars

Less than 3 cars to clear

Light

2 cars

9 car lengths over all

Reverse switch

Load compensator (potentiometer)

One of the very last models John built was the tiny layout of the Gorre Live Steamers, which ran under the arch of the original stone viaduct at Gorre. The track gauge of the non-operating layout was a mere two millimeters, but the HO scale club members all seemed to enjoy themselves. Russ Cain, one of the G.D. operators, took this photo of it.

The Timesaver. —— In 1966 John invented a model railroad switching game that he called the "Timesaver." The game consisted of a platform 10″ wide by 56″ long, on which John built a simple track arrangement with just five switches (later, he added another switch so that two Timesavers could be connected back-to-back for a more complex game). John's article about the Timesaver appeared in the November 1972 MODEL RAILROADER, and in the years since many modelers have built copies for themselves.

With the addition of a power supply, reversing switch, locomotive, and only five freight cars, the plain board with track became a challenging puzzle. John wrote, "After years of use, this little switching game has shown itself to have more variety and appeal than I ever thought possible." G.D. operator Don Mitchell added, "John liked the Timesaver almost as much as his big layout. He spent a lot of time with it."

The object of the game is to move the freight cars from their start positions to predetermined finish positions in the least time. Since the speed of the locomotive is fixed, the contestant who works steadily and efficiently, not necessarily the fellow who uses the least number of moves, is usually the winner. The regular G.D. operating crew usually played the game over coffee at the end of the session, and when they traveled to an NMRA meet, the game went along. It's more difficult than it looks, and Joe Cain told me that one of the first fellows to try it sat down, worked the puzzle for about five minutes, then got up and said: "Damn you John!"

John staged this photo and another like it as a hoax to convince other modelers that someone was building a working railroad in tiny 1/400 scale. In reality the models were HO, and the pencil and ruler were much-enlarged photos instead of the actual objects.

Andy Sperandeo recalls: "My first shot at running the Timesaver didn't come until I'd learned enough about it to win a pot, but I hadn't learned it well enough to avoid taking 45 minutes for what should have taken 10. Even when I got the hang of it, it was still disconcerting to be right in the

Squawbottom station, with its beautiful "witch's hat" cupola, was one of the last structures John added to the railroad. Jim Findley did much of the work, including an odd chimney which could be moved up or down to confound John!

middle of it and have John quietly say to someone else, 'Oh, I don't think I'd have done *that*.'"

The Allen sense of humor. —— We've already learned how John put a dinosaur to work on his model railroad, how he staged an elaborate joke (and poked fun at himself) with a pair of HO scale fat men, and how he hid a laugh box under the layout to ensure that operating sessions included occasional comic relief. While there are dozens of humorous anec-

This station at Angels Camp was also a late addition to the G.D. It shared a family resemblance with Squawbottom and Cross Junction. Don Mitchell took this photo not long before John's death.

dotes about John, one of his most imaginative jokes involved a complicated scheme to convince the model railroad press that someone was building and operating a model railroad in 1/400 scale, almost five times smaller than HO.

Late in 1971, using the name "Robert Thomas," John sent letters to MODEL RAILROADER, the NMRA *Bulletin*, and *Railroad Model Craftsman*, explaining that his job required that he travel frequently, and as a result he was building a 1/400 scale model railroad. He carefully photographed several coins, a pencil, a ruler, and two of his own fingers, then enlarged them to a size that would make his regular HO models appear much smaller by comparison. Next he cut out the enlarged photographs and positioned them and his models under identical lighting, re-photographing the whole scene. While John dropped the ruse after only four letters, it certainly was convincing.

John didn't mind an occasional joke on himself, or a prank that backfired. One of his more mischievous tricks nearly disrupted the whole railroad. He mounted a strong magnet lengthwise inside each of two cars in such a way that the cars would either attract or repel each other, making it impossible to uncouple or couple them, depending on which way they were oriented. What John hadn't planned on was that when the cars passed each other at a siding, they jumped sideways toward each other, derailing both trains.

Jim Findley, whose name has appeared often in these pages, was one of John's best model railroading friends. Jim, a retired serviceman, lived in Korea but visited John two or three times a year, usually building a new structure for the railroad or just helping out generally. During one of Jim's visits John decided the G.D. needed a better station at Squawbottom.

Jim recalls the project: "I made the chimney so it could telescope up and down, because John couldn't make up his mind how tall it should be. He'd say: 'That chimney needs to be a little shorter,' or 'just a little longer,' so I made a hole in the roof that was an exact fit for the chimney, and covered the entire length of the chimney with brick paper. That way, I could slide it up or down. Oh, I had a lot of fun with that. I set its length where John thought it ought to be, then I kept inching it up until one day John exclaimed, 'You made that chimney too darned long!'

"Then I'd take the station to the workbench, and after enough time had elapsed that John would think I'd done the work, I'd push the chimney down to where John thought he wanted it and bring the structure back to the layout. Throughout the next week I'd gradually push the chimney down until John thought I'd made it too short. He never did find out about the telescoping feature."

Once, Findley volunteered to clean John's stove, and while he was doing so, guests came and John took them downstairs to see the railroad. The guests didn't know Jim, so he played a trick that made John furious, if only for a moment. After finishing the stove, Findley went downstairs and said, "I've finished cleaning your stove, Mr. Allen, now can I play with your trains?"

On yet another occasion when a visitor was present, John asked Jim to help him fix something on the railroad. Later, when the three went out to dinner together, the guest told Findley right in front of John: "I don't know what John pays you, but I'll double the pay if you'll come and help fix my railroad." "Twice nothing is still nothing," snorted John.

As a short freight works slowly upgrade out of Eagle's Nest, it's easy to imagine that this scene was photographed in the high Sierras or the Rockies instead of in the basement of a modest home near the Pacific coast. Such was the magic of the Wizard of Monterey.

The model railroad artist. —— Many people have asked me why John Allen became so well known and respected—almost to the point of awe—as a model railroader. I think there were three reasons. First was his personality. While John could and did irritate people at times, his purpose was always to help them toward the twin goals of better modeling and better operation. To my knowledge, while he disliked sloppy performance, he did not dislike any of his fellow model railroaders.

Second, while others were as accomplished in model railroading as John, he had the ability and desire to show his work to others with beautifully composed and lit photographs. Even model railroaders who disliked John's ideas or techniques could not help but appreciate the ability so clearly shown by his pictures.

Finally, John adopted a middle-of-the-road concept for his railroad. He strove for—and achieved—good overall effect rather than devoting his time to superdetailing on the one hand, or extreme caricature on the other. He was willing to use illusion to achieve effects that meticulous inch-for-inch modeling could not, and also was willing to concoct a yarn to explain away an incongruity.

For John Allen, model railroading was an art as well as a hobby and craft. His brother Andrew summed up John about as well as it will ever be done when he told me: "His main object in life was to do something he thought was creative. Whether he made money from it or not wasn't essential, as long as he had enough to live off. He didn't work for anyone else, but he worked three times as hard creating the railroad as he might have on a job."

Epilogue

JOHN ALLEN died of a heart attack on the evening of January 6, 1973. As if to compound the tragedy, only ten days after John's death fire gutted the house at 9 Cielo Vista Terrace, utterly destroying his fabulous Gorre & Daphetid.

John, who had suffered at least one serious heart attack in the 1960s, was not feeling well in the fall of 1972, yet he worked energetically to finish the G.D. main line. During a phone conversation he told me he thought the "Golden Spike" might be driven in April or May of 1973, and that I should plan to visit then. On October 13, 1972, he wrote to Jim Findley: "Been pushing the line up from Great Divide to Angels Camp. All track and bridges are in, but I still have the [uncoupling] ramps to install. The work goes slowly, and it takes me two or three times as long to do something as 10 years ago. Losing or gaining no weight but still run out of breath awful easy. Don't sleep too well at night but maybe it's because I do [sleep] some during day."

The possibility of a fatal heart attack may have been on John's mind when he continued: "Don't know what to do with the house and railroad. You are the only one who might use it, but I'm not sure you'd want the care of it and the railroad. I see no sense in leaving it to anyone who won't take the trouble to find out how it works, and even I am beginning to forget too much that is necessary. If I have a couple more years, even at my reduced efficiency, I think I can get the main line done and operating for a short time as I planned 19 years ago."

Jim Findley was visiting when John passed away, and he stayed in the house for a few days after John's death. Andrew Allen and his wife visited daily to inventory John's effects and search for a will. The G.D. operators discussed various ways to preserve the railroad, and the family was amenable. "One of the things John wanted," Earl Flaws recalled, "was that we keep the railroad in operating condition. He hoped someone could keep the railroad going." Bill Corsa added: "We would all have chipped in for it." Joe Cain thought

about buying the house, and Jim Findley told me he would be willing to stay there. Darrell Harbin was single and could have served as the caretaker. The fire ended all such possibilities.

The G.D. operators were very helpful to the family, and on their regular operating night, Tuesday, January 16, 1973, Andrew invited them to come and operate the railroad. The session was over before 11:00, and since the house was to remain vacant that night, before leaving the crew turned off all power to the layout and lighting, shut down the gas water heater, and adjusted the floor furnace thermostat to 65 degrees to keep the railroad dry.

Around midnight a neighbor noticed sparks and smoke coming from the house and called the Monterey Fire Department. Help arrived quickly, but too late to save the railroad. The initial assessment was that the fire was caused by "electric wiring of the model railroad," but a private fire investigator commissioned by Andrew Allen later determined that the gas floor furnace in the Helengon Gap alcove was the culprit. John had hardly ever used this furnace, mostly because he liked to keep the house cool, but also perhaps because he knew the furnace was improperly vented to the outside.

In 1974 Andrew Allen asked if I would go to Monterey and see if the railroad could be saved in any way. Could it—or perhaps part of it—be moved to a museum? Could it be rebuilt on the spot? I was happy to oblige, and it occurred to me that if John's photos had not burned, a book about him might still be possible.

When we arrived at the house, it was apparent almost immediately that the layout was in no condition to restore. The fire had completely demolished many areas, and the few scenes that were recognizable were terribly charred; the beauty was gone. We tried to save the famous French Gulch section, but after two hours of sawing and sweating it collapsed as we moved it away from the wall.

In the darkroom I found John's negatives, and up-

In this moonlit scene at Andrews, G.D. Shay 7 shuffles cars along the millpond siding. The tiny stone building on the left, "Linn's Archives, Literature and Altered Articles," was a gentle joke aimed at me. It referred to my habit of extensively rewriting articles that John (and others) submitted to MODEL RAILROADER magazine while I was Editor.

stairs were his correspondence files, drawings, and planning notebooks, including the manuscripts of published and future articles. Those materials, added to John's color slides (which had been rescued earlier and were the property of Andrew Allen), made it possible to produce this book. It is my hope that for years to come many model railroaders will enjoy knowing about John Allen, perhaps the greatest thinker this hobby will ever have.

We miss you, John.

ABOUT THE AUTHOR

When Linn H. Westcott retired in 1978 after a 43-year career in model railroad publishing, his enthusiasm for his hobby remained undiminished. Linn had served on the staffs of MODEL RAILROADER magazine, TRAINS magazine, MODEL TRAINS magazine, and Kalmbach Books. After 16 years as Editor, Linn became *Editor Emeritus* of MODEL RAILROADER in 1977. His numerous contributions to the hobby include innovations in track planning, wiring, train control, scenery, and benchwork. Many of Linn's ideas found commercial application; all were tested on MODEL RAILROADER magazine's project railroads and his own HO scale Sunset Railway & Navigation Co. layout.

Linn's other books include INTRODUCTION TO SCALE MODEL RAILROADING, HOW TO WIRE YOUR MODEL RAILROAD, HOW TO BUILD MODEL RAILROAD BENCHWORK, HO RAILROAD THAT GROWS, 101 TRACK PLANS FOR MODEL RAILROADERS, HO PRIMER, TRACK PLANS FOR SECTIONAL TRACK, and MODEL RAILROADER CYCLOPEDIA, VOLUME 1, STEAM LOCOMOTIVES.

Linn died in September 1980, while preparing the manuscript for this book about his friend John Allen.

ABOUT THE QUOTATIONS

As Linn wrote in his Foreword (page 2), much of the text of this book is in John Allen's own words, and in a very real sense this is the book that John intended to write, but never did. The quotations come from many sources, including John's voluminous personal correspondence, the original manuscripts for his magazine articles, and notes for two books he never finished: "This is a Model Railroad," and "Model Railroad Scenery."

Footnotes, a bibliography, and other scholarly notation would serve no useful purpose in this book, so I've omitted the derivation in most instances where John is quoted. Where the context is important to the discussion I've included a reference in the text or caption.

Bob Hayden
Kalmbach Publishing Co.
April, 1981